Note to

The statements presented in this book are my own opinions based on life experiences and introspection. I routinely use 1st person references such as "I recommend, I suggest, etc." and 2nd person references such as "you should, you need, etc." for ease of readability and writing. These, and all other statements in this book, should not be taken as personal investment advice, nor do any statements guarantee that you will achieve a certain investment performance if implemented.

Any historical data, calculations, charts, or graphs presented in this text are solely to provide a visual illustration of my opinions and do not specifically state or imply any sort of investment recommendation in any specific security. Calculations, though intended to be accurate and representative, cannot be guaranteed as such.

Participating in the stock market is inherently risky and can result in immediate and substantial losses. Before making any investments, you should consult with a personal investment advisor to obtain advice tailored to your specific circumstances. I solely represent myself as a publisher, not as an investment advisor or being in the business of providing investment advice. In no event shall I be liable for any results due to actions taken from statements in this book.

Like all information you will come across in life, you are encouraged to understand the viewpoints presented in this book and then decide as to how, or if, you will use them. Never blindly follow one person's opinions.

Stay smart,

Philip Fanara

www.predictingsociety.com

Written by Philip Fanara

Edited by Steve Ure
Cover design by Kelly Stahley

Contents

A Not So Average Introduction

If you are so good at investing, why write a book?

Publishing quality would skyrocket if more readers would ask this question before purchasing an investing book. This applies to any publishing – if the author is so good at what he is writing about, then why does he spend the time writing about it at all?

Most authors do not answer this question, either because they lack the integrity to be transparent with their readers, or they lack the insight to truly understand their own motivation.

If the author has the insight but not the integrity to disclose his true motivation in writing the book, how can you trust anything he later says?

Or if the author does not have the insight to understand his motivation for writing the book, how does he have sufficient insight to provide meaningful advice to the reader?

The fact is: everything we do, every action we take, benefits us in some manner.

This is a rather difficult concept for most people to handle. Some would point to the likes of famous philanthropists such as Bill Gates, who donated billions of dollars to impoverished countries. Donating billions of dollars to Africa has to be a selfless act, right?

False. Donations of any sort, whether it be money, time, or advice, give the donor a satisfaction that he is making a difference in the world. Oddly enough, money is the most solicited but least donated item; while advice is the least solicited but most frequently donated item. Can you guess why?

Everybody has his or her own source of pleasure. For one person it may be commanding a Fortune 500 company, for another it may be motivating a department of three A/R clerks to shave one more day off the billing cycle. Some would rather ditch work and travel the world, while others prefer to live in a small town and raise two children that will surely grow up to be a doctor and a lawyer.

Philanthropists are no different. They receive pleasure from helping others live a more comfortable life. Another (maybe less politically) way to put it, they perform selfless acts that selfishly benefit themselves.

Please do not misinterpret my intentions; I am not disparaging philanthropists. Disparaging anyone's source of pleasure would convey a fundamental misunderstanding of the concept I just described. I am merely providing you with the basic philosophy needed to understand concepts later discussed in this book.

So going back to our original question – "If you are so good at investing, why write a book?"

I wrote this book to overcome the same hurdle that most investors have: a lack of starting capital needed to break away from society's confines and live comfortably off smart investment decisions. Ironically, to get rich in the stock market you need to already be rich, or invest for years to get the wheels of compounding interest rolling along.

Imagine two different investors. One is an ignorant investor who inherited $10 million; the other is a smart middle-class investor who has saved $10 thousand. The ignorant investor will earn much more money by going all-in on Treasury bonds than the smart investor will earn through superb investment decisions.

In fact, if the ignorant investor earns 3% every year and the smart investor earns 20% every year, it would take 35 years before the smart investor began earning more money per year than the ignorant investor. Even more upsetting, it would take 47 years before he had more *total dollars* than the ignorant investor.

Since I have neither the privilege of already being rich nor the desire to invest for 35 years before realizing significant returns, I will gladly trade my stock market insight with thousands of readers for a head start in the investment world.

If you share the same philosophy, I urge you to find your launching pad – whether that be a high paying job, starting a successful business, or writing a book on your expertise. You will get rich much quicker in the stock market if you can begin the journey with a hundred thousand dollars versus one thousand dollars.

To thank you for supporting my launching pad, I will help you receive many times your money's worth from this book.

Specifically, my goal is for you to retire from your normal job in 4 years as a millionaire, allowing you to spend time working from home as an investor. From there you can choose to either fully retire, or continue your insightful investing and possibly become a billionaire in less than 15 years later.

Yes, this does sound like a lofty goal, however it is very practical, as explained in detail throughout the book.

This book will provide you with a deep critical look into stock market psychology. It offers insight that is relatively unknown throughout the investment community, yet is practical enough so that you can apply the exact same methodologies if you so choose.

The reason why most people do not become rich in the market is the same reason why most people do not become rich in any area of life. They do not have the insight to understand how the world works and the creativity to form a niche for themselves.

Life experiences guide your future. The key to becoming successful in life is to find out how to best utilize your experiences to fill a niche.

From birth until now, my life experiences have guided me towards acquiring skills necessary to write this book. Some skills I purposely pursued and others I did not even seek out. It is irrelevant whether you learn skills by choice or by chance. The important fact is that you take a critical look at your own skills and determine how you can use them to become successful.

I am using this book to transfer my knowledge to you. I will not keep anything to myself nor will I add unnecessary filler to artificially inflate the number of pages. The same cannot be said about most authors out there (think of how many times you purchased a 250-page book that could have been written in 25 pages).

I will not censor my thoughts or try to play both sides of the field. I will tell you if I believe a certain investment strategy to be worthless, and give you the reason why. Being so direct will inevitably offend a few softies in some form or fashion, and I confidently predict they will punish me by writing a scathing one-star review or sending an email containing words they would never use in public. Although undesirable, I will gladly accept this as a cost of retaining my dignity as an author, knowing that I did not censor myself in order to appeal to the mainstream public.

You will reap the benefits by receiving a spectacular book that has been targeted towards a core group of investors – those with the intelligence and self-control to act as an outsider peering in to the market, using its fluctuations and irrationality to your advantage, rather than the majority of investors who let the market control them.

Remember – those who are successful in life are not slaves to their environment, they shape their own environment.

I hope you enjoy this book and wish you exceptional success.

Part I – There is no normal: Human nature and its relation to stock market failure

An individual can be easily manipulated if he or she perceives the current situation to be a repeat of a past situation.

Associating false stimuli to responses

In the early 20th century, Ivan Pavlov, a Russian physiologist, published observations on what is now known as *classical conditioning*. Classical conditioning is the psychological effect of applying a cause-and-effect relationship to unrelated stimuli.

Pavlov initially conducted experiments on dogs, ringing a bell immediately before feeding them. After repeating his procedure a few times, the dogs began to salivate when the bell was rung. Therefore the dogs began to *expect* food when hearing a bell because these two stimuli happened to be paired together in the past.

Humans are not above falling prey to this behavior, as much as we would like to think that we are.

One example arises from my early job as a charity bingo caller. Charity bingo? Well, outside of Indian reservations, gambling is illegal in Louisiana. Gambling for charity is not, however. The difference?

In normal gambling, all the profits go to the business owners; in charity gambling all the profits go to a designated charity... after "expenses" have been paid.

Expenses primarily include a hefty chunk of money to the bingo hall owner that could easily place him in a top income tax bracket. And of course expenses also include the bingo winnings and our salaries, as meager as they were.

So in the government's opinion, gambling is a tax on the poor and should be kept out of society. However if there is a feel-good cause behind gambling, then, sure, we are fine with taxing the poor.

The primary patrons of this charity bingo were older, poorer women. They would walk in with the same sour scowl plastered underneath a bushel of dark moustache fuzz, pink hair rollers securely locked in place, wearing loose-fitting moo-moo dresses, puffing on a generic brand cigarette.

We would sell as many $5 bingo cards to them as they wanted to buy. The idea is the more cards you play, the more of a chance you have to win. These women quickly learned that in order to get a leg-up on the competition, they simply had to buy more cards than the other women.

So, if the normal bingo player uses one card, then buying two cards will double their chance of winning. Not wanting to be left behind, the one-card players also started buying two. To keep that same advantage over the competition, the two-card players started buying three.

This vicious circle continued until all the players were playing three to four cards each. This interclass competition only hurt the bingo players (who were already playing a very low yielding game based on chance) because they were now competing against each other as well as the "house" – all while giving us more money for no additional payout.

There were a couple of hard-nosed women who would not budge from playing one card. Instead they had a more elegant strategy: shouting out for me to call numbers faster so that the women playing multiple cards could not keep up.

Some used other interesting methods to gain leverage over their opponents. One woman kept a pink-haired troll doll facing her the entire time, which was sure to tip luck her way. Another had a custom-made denim bingo bag with dozens of different colored markers; each one of these markers would be used in a specific sequence.

After calling hundreds of bingo games, I am confident that these women did not have a statistical advantage over those that played the game with no observable gimmicks. So why would they continue spending energy on these frivolous activities?

Because they had all experienced an occasion where they won a game while performing these activities.

They attributed every win thereafter to this secret formula, while every loss was conveniently blamed on outside interference and quickly forgotten.

Humans have an innate desire to assign causes to responses; this behavior helps us learn from past situations to increase our chance of future survivability. Unfortunately, evolution did not consider that this behavior hurts us when playing bingo.

When humans participate in an activity with random outcomes, they tend to assign a wide variety of ridiculous causes to responses.

I may be picking on bingo players now, but the same principle applies to businesspeople, even though they may not admit or even be aware of it. Interestingly, a well-known businessman has been rumored to attribute his success to his infamous hairstyle.

Classical conditioning dictates our lives as well. We wear a specific suit to an important meeting based on our previous luck with that suit. We order and drink some sort of concoction of sugar, milk, flavoring, and a pinch of coffee tailored to such stringent specifications that, like a snowflake, there is none other like it. We use the same brand of toothpaste for years because we never had a cavity since switching to it – the list goes on.

If society attaches such insignificant stimuli to those responses, imagine the kind of stimuli that dictates people's investment techniques! This is the reason that the stock market is so unpredictable and appears to move randomly.

Most investment "strategies" you read about are really just sophisticated (and unnecessarily complex) versions of the bingo lady's troll doll.

The stock market – random or not?

The stock market itself is not random. It may appear to move in a random fashion, however if you personally knew everybody that traded a particular stock, specifically their personalities and current financial situations, then you could predict movements of that stock much more accurately than an individual without this knowledge. When the quantity of available information affects one's ability to predict a future outcome, then the outcome is not truly random.

Let us put this in a tangible perspective.

What is a good price-to-book ratio? An average investor may say anything within the 1-3 range; a fundamental investor may say anything less than 1; a technical trader may say that it does not matter. These individuals each associate a certain P/B ratio to their previous success. And guess what? They were all correct at a particular time. Then who is correct overall? Does P/B even matter?

The answer depends on the situation. Some securities can trade at low P/B ratios for years while others trade at high ratios for years. This frustrates a fundamental investor, who, upon finding a stock trading at such a low P/B ratio, buys into the stock with voluptuous swagger because he knows the market will soon realize its true value.

Days turn into weeks, weeks into months, months into years, and the stock has still not budged upwards. The fundamentalist curses other investors for not taking advantage of this wonderful buy-in opportunity, all while his money erodes away in a non-performing stock.

This investor made the all-too-common mistake of applying a blanket rule to a specific stock. In effect, he made a decision with such confidence as if he personally knew the entire investment community, their personalities, and their financial situations.

The technical trader laughs at the failed fundamentalist, then proceeds to make a different, but equally wrong assumption, on her next trade. Instead of observing a low P/B ratio as the buy-in point, she swears that this stock has just made an inverse head-and-shoulders pattern that suspiciously resembles the Aquarius zodiac, which is her own zodiac sign. You see Mr. Fundamentalist, this is how smart investing is done. She proceeds to invest her entire portfolio in this stock and waits for the uptrend.

Of course, the uptrend does not come; instead, the stock crashes 30% down after her large investment and never recovers for years.

The unfortunate truth is that in these, and in most cases, investors never learn where they went wrong. In fact, they will continue performing faulty strategies and will continue attributing negative results to external stimuli. You have the advantage of exploiting this spectacle for your personal gain, as long as you do not fall prey to it yourself.

Those who never learn, never succeed

Not learning from one's mistakes is due to *confirmation bias*, and it occurs in all aspects of life. People only take in those facts that align with their beliefs; any opposing facts are disregarded. Confirmation bias is especially dangerous because people do it unconsciously. Before risking your life savings in the market, you need to ensure that you are not blinded by your own confirmation bias.

How do you do this? Many quick-witted individuals suggest creating a strict set of trading rules that should always be followed. Yes, this is true to an extent. However, merely *following* a set of trading rules is not what leads to market success; you must *possess* the insight necessary to create valuable rules.

One can create all the rules he wants. If the rules are worthless, his portfolio will be worthless. This is the area where many quick-witted people fall short.

Wit and insightfulness are often on opposite ends of each other. Quick-witted individuals, while entertaining to converse with, often jump to conclusions without adequate support.

Many (not all) executives achieve such a high-level position through wit and personality rather than insightfulness (come to think of it, the same applies to many successful authors). This is not a problem if the executive solely functions as the company's likeable face. Problems occur when the executive is expected to make decisions that can easily break the company. If the executive does not have an insightful team behind her, then decisions come about with little rhyme or reason. Others in the company do not challenge her opinions – out of respect, fear, or ignorance.

Even a small decision coming from the top will ripple downward through the company's channels, affecting processes that in turn affect other processes, and so on. This is referred to as the *chaos theory*, which totes the philosophy that simple acts such as a butterfly flapping its wings can lead to a series of growing events that eventually cause a hurricane on the other end of the world. Unlike butterflies, we as humans have the ability to think through our decisions before acting upon them. The problem is that we do not always take advantage of this ability.

Because the quick-witted executive makes decisions on a whim without regard to their potential impacts, the company's profitability is slowly eaten away. No one is able to point out the root cause because the bad decision is whitewashed through so many people and processes before decreasing profits are observed – similar to how no one can trace a hurricane's origins to a specific butterfly.

We should be fair here and realize that the executive is not always to blame – it is difficult to fully grasp the effect her decision will have on an entire company. This is an inherent flaw in all business structures. We keep promoting the top performers until they are no longer in a position to do what they were originally good at.

The only way to avoid confirmation bias without constantly playing devil's advocate to yourself (and therefore going insane) is to accept the fact that there is no perfect buy-in opportunity out there. In certain situations, you may be able to tilt the probability in your favor; however, the unknown element (the ten-sigma event, black swan, whatever you would like to call it) will always lurk out there and pose a risk to your financial portfolio.

Once you accept the fact that there are no perfect buy-in opportunities – that there is no normal – you are ready to take the first step in exploiting society's weaknesses in the stock market.

Part II – Stocks are not marriage material: Insightful thinking and its relation to stock market success

For better or worse, richer or poorer, sickness and in health, until death do us part... shall I hold onto this stock

Skill or Luck?

I have witnessed some interesting behaviors while studying stock market psychology. One of the most comedic examples is an investor's willingness to hold onto a stock no matter what the situation. An investor will give his stock more leeway before leaving it than he would give to own his wife. This method of holding stocks "forever" was made famous by Warren Buffett. In the 1980s, he was even bold enough to name specific stocks of Berkshire Hathaway that he would never sell, no matter the situation.

This was not the first time Buffett made such a statement. Before becoming a diversified investment management company, and for the majority of its life, Berkshire Hathaway was a textile manufacturing company. Buffett began acquiring Berkshire Hathaway shares in the 1960s when the textile industry as a whole was losing market share to cheaper, overseas textile companies. He eventually acquired enough shares to boot the existing management team out and transform it into the acquisition vehicle it is today.

Thankfully Buffett is human like us – imagine if he had been born a parasite instead. With his outstanding success of latching onto a host, taking over its bodily functions, and exponentially growing so large that it was able to gobble up huge chunks of Wells Fargo, General Motors, Wal-Mart, The Washington Post, IBM, Coca-Cola, American Express…. Well, we are just fortunate he was born a human!

The transition from a low profitable textile company to a high profitable company gobbler was a rather awkward one. During the height of the transition in the 1970s, Buffett made several comments acknowledging that the textile business was not as profitable as Berkshire's other holdings, however he still believed that Berkshire should retain the business.

At the time, his reasons for keeping the textile business were because its operations kept many people employed, management was energetic and straightforward in its approach to the problems, and that there was reasonable expectation that profits could improve in the future.

These expectations never panned out. Berkshire Hathaway gave up trying to revitalize the textile operations and completely shut it down in 1985. Buffett later admitted that purchasing the original Berkshire Hathaway textile business was his worst investment mistake.

Ironically, only one year later in 1986, Buffett boldly claimed that Berkshire would permanently hold stock in three companies: Capital Cities/ABC Inc., GEICO Corporation, and The Washington Post. Yes, the same person, who just finished admitting that he had wrongly blinded himself for years, was now so convinced in his investing ability that he swore never to sell specific stocks.

To Buffett's credit, Berkshire Hathaway still owns these three stocks. However, any of these could have easily turned into another case of the textile operation, whereby an outdated business model is replaced with stiffer competition elsewhere. And moreover, these three stocks did not consistently outperform all other stocks in the market. Buffett became so convinced and comfortable in his position that he passed over better moneymaking opportunities elsewhere.

No one is a fortuneteller. The great businesses of today will not be the great businesses of tomorrow. However many people still trust their life savings in the hands of a few large businesses; they believe that these companies will be around forever. Think of Standard Oil, RCA, Compaq, General Foods, MCI, Pan Am, and Montgomery Ward – back in their prime no one would bet that these companies would be dissolved or acquired for pennies on the dollar.

Just as Buffett made the mistake of foregoing better returns elsewhere by stubbornly holding positions, many investors fall victim to holding stocks much longer than they should. Why do they not want to let go of a profitable stock?

First off, letting go would mean starting over. After selecting a stock that happens to perform well in the short-term, investors fool themselves into believing they have found a diamond in the rough. The more time the investor spent researching the stock, the more complex his selection methodology, or the more familiar he is with management, then the stronger his belief is. The investor assumes that he has sufficiently paid his dues and is being rewarded through significant gains. So he holds on to the stock.

Let us consider a situation that occurs every day. A middle-aged investor with plans to retire in five years (but desires to retire now) has purchased a software stock he believes is destined to be the next Microsoft.

Two days pass with the investor proudly holding onto his future retirement ticket, already up 15% from his cost basis in such a short time. He proudly touts his noteworthy foresight to friends and family – suggesting they should get in before the price skyrockets up.

Then one morning he wakes up, and to his horror, the stock dropped 10% after opening! No news was released – how could this happen?

There are many reasons this could happen, most of which we cannot predict. As discussed in Part I, investors fool themselves into believing they can predict everyone's actions within the market. They forget that the stock market is not physics; there is no set of rules that correctly predicts future market activity. They also forget that no company is infallible; any stock price can drop like a rock for no apparent reason.

It does not matter that a stock is trading at an exasperatedly low P/B, or has made the strongest inverse head-and-shoulders pattern seen in ages. The fact is that placing too much credit in your analysis or the supposed laws of the market will only make you more of a slave to the market. Being a slave means you are not in control of your portfolio. You are allowing other traders to dictate your financial health.

Going back to our example – after being shocked at the 10% loss at opening, the investor feels the sudden urge to put more money into this stock. He tells himself that it is bound to bounce back up and this is a great buying opportunity. Therefore he sells some of his other holdings at a small loss and purchases more of his prodigal stock.

An hour later the stock falls another 10%, then 5% an hour after that. Our investor is down 10% from his first cost basis and 15% down from his second basis. Watching his hard-earned money disintegrate in front of him, the investor begins becoming irrational. Nervously shaking and sweating, he goes into a frantic panic, liquidating all other securities to purchase more of this stock.

Consciously, he assures himself that the stock is a great value buy; unconsciously he is just yearning to lower his cost basis to turn that red number into a green number. In effect, he has now placed his entire financial portfolio in the hands of thousands of faceless investors in cyberspace.

The stock price never recovers to its original cost basis. Unable to bring himself to reality and sell the stock, it trends downward for three years until Microsoft acquires it at a bargain price (the investor was very insightful in one aspect, it did not just become the *next* Microsoft, it *became* Microsoft). Our investor receives 10 cents on the dollar back from his average cost basis. Years of hard work down the drain.

This bleak scenario is a frequent, but preventable occurrence in the stock market. There are three lessons to learn here: 1) Never fool yourself into believing that you have picked the perfect stock, no matter what kind of reasoning you had for picking it; 2) Never place over 10% of your net worth in one stock, no matter how attractive it looks; and 3) Take small, 3% gains as soon as they come.

That's right, I am saying that stocks should be sold once they surpass 3% of the cost basis.

Where do I get the nerve to make such a bold statement, when billionaires like Warren Buffett advocate holding stocks forever? Well, remember that you and I are not Warren Buffett, and trading like him will not make us billionaires as well.

Going back to the concept of classical conditioning described in Part I, people falsely associate their success to unrelated stimuli. If Warren Buffett became rich holding stocks forever, what strategy do you think he would recommend to becoming rich? Holding stocks forever. If George Soros, the world's richest hedge fund manager, was asked the same question, what would his response be? Hedge funds trading at maximum leverage. What about a famous technical trader? You guessed it, technical analysis.

You must understand one extremely important fact: many traders did not become successful by figuring out the laws of the market. Many became successful because of statistical law; therefore mimicking their strategies will certainly not produce the same success.

Society's focus on luck, not skill

Nassim Nicholas Taleb beautifully describes this concept in his book, *Fooled by Randomness: The Hidden Role of Chance in Life and in the Markets*. Taleb makes the interesting point that if you had an infinite amount of monkeys on typewriters randomly clapping away, that one of them would type an exact version of the *Iliad*.

This particular monkey would be called a genius, paraded around on television, studied, and forever remembered as the greatest monkey that ever lived. If this monkey could speak, he would attribute his remarkable success to his strict upbringing, God, and his habit of eating only unripe bananas. Soon all monkeys would begin raising their offspring in strict, religious households that only purchased unripe bananas.

We would never hear of the countless other monkeys that typed gibberish, yet were also raised in strict, religious households that purchased unripe bananas – they were not lucky enough to have randomly typed the Iliad. Likewise, we would never hear about other successful monkeys who happened to be raised in lax, non-religious households that only purchased overripe bananas; these monkeys were not lucky enough to be an extreme outlier.

Revisiting my original statement, you cannot expect to become a successful investor by mimicking the strategies of a successful investor. Too many variables occurred that were outside of the successful trader's control, yet still contributed to his miraculous success.

Millions of people have studied and emulated prosperous investors like Warren Buffett and have not come close to his investing achievements. This is because as smart as Buffett is, he does not hold a magical secret to investing. In fact, it is possible that his success is not solely due to his strategy, but that he implemented his strategy at the perfect time. Or another way to think about it, he was *born* at the perfect time, in the perfect place, and in the perfect environment.

Believe it or not, we do not have much (if any) control over who we become in adulthood. Modern science attributes our actions to either genetics or the environment. If this is correct, then are we really in control of our life?

We certainly do not choose our genetics. We do have the ability to change our environment after reaching a certain maturity. However, this decision is based on a combination of our genetics and the environment we were raised into. Therefore we are not actually exercising free will, but merely performing actions dictated by factors outside our control.

What if Warren Buffett's father never owned a brokerage company – would he have still taken such an interest in the stock market? What if he was born in a lower-class family – would he have been exposed to business at such a young age? What if Benjamin Graham had never been born – would Buffett have ever learned and applied Graham's analysis techniques?

If you understand this philosophical concept, then you must agree that there are people, both living and dead, who would have been extremely effective traders had they been put in the correct situation. Possibly these people grew up in the correct environment but did not have the genetic capability; or vice-versa, they had the genetic capability but did not grow up in the correct environment.

There could be a homeless man somewhere holding a sign at the city's longest red-light intersection who knows nothing about investing, however if he had just been born to different parents then he would have been the most successful trader alive. After all, he is insightful enough to figure out that the best intersection to beg for money is the one with the longest red light. With so many market participants, statistical laws guarantee that some will become extreme outliers because of luck.

The same concept applies to the lottery. So many people participate in it that although the odds are overwhelmingly stacked against the players, eventually someone will win. Everyone asks the winner for her secret. She proudly touts that her strategy was playing the numbers corresponding to her children's ages. This influences other participants to begin playing their children's ages, which of course does not result in more winners. Lots of mimicking that never results in success. Sound familiar?

Warren Buffett's strategy is widely known and followed throughout the investment community, yet there is still only one Warren Buffett alive. The key point is that you should think through your investment strategy for reasonableness. Do not blindly follow one person's advice because she struck it rich in the market nor discredit another person's advice because he did not strike it rich. I urge you to even apply this advice to statements in this book – make sure what I am telling you is sensible and based on reasonable assumptions before you personally apply it.

You still want to know how I could possibly recommend never holding a stock past 3% gain over the cost basis. Patience, my Padawan, one does not become a wine connoisseur by simply swallowing a lot of wine, but by making a focused effort to understand the subtle differences in wine.

Think yourself out of problems

I have spent my entire professional career as an internal auditor, first for a large Fortune 500 company, and then a small and quickly growing family-owned company. Across all types of organizations, internal auditors can be best described as consultants whose job is to help management identify and control risk.

Companies are filled with various risks. Internal auditors are responsible for assessing and providing recommendations to mitigate these risks, whether they relate to efficient/effective operations, accuracy of the company's financial statements, government compliance, safety – you name it. If something poses a significant risk to the organization, it is fair game for an internal auditor.

In order to identify and help mitigate risks, auditors must be familiar with how the entire company works. How long does it take to become familiar with every single process that occurs in a company? The answer should be obvious. An auditor never becomes familiar with every single process that occurs in a company.

Think back to how you felt the first day in your current position compared to how you now feel in this position. You are much more comfortable now because you are familiar with your daily processes.

Auditors never become familiar with the entire company's processes because they do not spend enough time learning a process before moving on to the next. Therefore, auditors never become comfortable in their job.

I am faced with a different problem every day I go to work. My job is to figure out a solution that not only solves the problem, but also is cost-effective and is accepted by management. This means going to management, who has spent the past 20+ years running their department, and telling them how they need to change – all while my experience is limited to the month or so spent researching their processes. Management is naturally resistant to change, which makes things all the more difficult. Imagine doing this every single day for years. Eventually you become skillful at solving seemingly impossible problems.

The reason I am telling you all this is because this type of work taught me the most valuable lesson in my entire life: <u>Any problem can be solved with insightful thinking</u>.

Realizing this concept can change your life, seriously.

Think of all the remarkable feats the human race has accomplished since becoming self-aware. We have evolved from a species dependent on its environment into a species that shapes its own environment. How did we do this? Why did we do this?

Humans are motivated by the need to survive. We possess genes that force us to fight for survival every single day of our lives. Fighting for survival 10,000 years ago meant defending your tribe against wild animals and other tribes; fighting for survival now means waking up early, driving to the office, and performing a specialized task for 8 hours.

Whether it is 10,000 years ago or today, in order to survive we have to spend a substantial portion of our life performing activities we would normally not be doing.

There is one substantial improvement we have made over the years. Ten thousand years ago, survival required quadruple the amount of time and energy than is required today. There were no nights and weekends off, your entire life was devoted to survival.

Now the modern human only needs to spend about 40 hours per week to survive. This allows us to spend more time performing self-satisfying activities, such as traveling, continuing education, and social interactions.

The human race was able to make this transition through insightful thinking. If early humans had simply accepted their problems, rather than strived for a better life, then we would have never progressed to where we are at now.

My career of constantly solving difficult problems in order to survive gave me the epiphany that <u>any problem can be solved with insightful thinking</u>.

I thought to myself, if it is true that any problem in the world can be solved, then how could I use this to my advantage?

Well, my greatest desire is freedom. Freedom to go wherever I want, live anywhere I want, wake up when I want, do anything I want, and have anything I want. All of these wants are self-satisfying activities that I currently cannot have because of time and capital constraints. In other words, I am spending too much time on survival activities than on self-satisfying activities.

I asked myself if it is ever possible to achieve my dream of complete freedom. Maybe so, but that may not come until retirement age after spending the better half of my life dominated by survival activities. Even the highest paid executives are still just trying to survive. They may have a slightly better survival/satisfaction balance, but in the end, they are spending the better part of their life surviving.

How does one achieve financial freedom quickly? You need a process that has the following characteristics:

First, it needs to be quick and easy to get into. A few highly paid executives may make hundreds of millions each year, but getting to that point could take 30-40 years and is not totally in your control.

Second, it needs to have a high probability of success. Winning a Powerball jackpot will certainly give one financial freedom, however it is near impossible to win. In fact, you have a higher chance of dying in a car crash on the way to buy the ticket than you do actually winning the jackpot.

Third, it needs to be a legal activity. It may be mildly humorous to point that out, however there are many ways to earn financial freedom where society has said "No-no, that is not an acceptable activity, Mr. Entrepreneur." Deviating from society's restrictions poses the risk that you will be caught and lose your chance at freedom. This causes one to live their life in constant fear of being caught, and if you live in constant fear, then what is the point of being financially free?

It did not take long to conclude that the stock market successfully meets all three criteria. It is quick and easy to get into; many online brokers will gladly take your commission fees. Investing can be an activity with a high probability of success – if you are smart about it. Lastly, it is a legal activity, although some people even find ways to mess that up.

The stock market is a sea of flowing cash; every day you sail out to sea, on a rickety boat with a small net, hoping to bring some money back. If you get greedy and venture out too far in hopes of nailing a huge catch, you will sink to the depths. If you are fearful and stay in shallow waters, you will live on minnows your whole life.

To become rich in the market you need to treat it for what it is: a sea of flowing cash. Do not get greedy and try to become rich in a few days, and do not be so fearful that you never participate in it.

Sail out a moderate distance and cast your small net. Catch the majority of the fish in that area, sail back home, and sell the fish to buy a bigger net. Over time, your net will be the size of a city.

Fear and greed

Hundreds of billions of dollars change hands in the stock market on a daily basis. With this huge amount of money moving around daily, the majority of investors never become rich in the stock market in their entire life. Why is this?

Fear and greed. Evolution has instilled emotions into us to ensure our physical survival in the wild; these same emotions hinder our survival in the stock market. Ten thousand years ago, survival meant *physically* surviving. Investing is not a physical activity, though; it is a *logical* activity.

Fear and greed cause your body to release situation-specific hormones. These hormones are perfect for ensuring physical survival, but are downright awful for logical survival. They actually cause you to perform worse in the market by diverting attention away from rational thinking and towards physical survival (fear) or ignorant euphoria (greed).

Greed causes stock marriages, as discussed in Part I. Fear causes panic selling and in some cases, panic buying.

Let us analyze the fear-related behaviors.

Why would someone panic sell? Because they are afraid to lose all their money.

What kind of people would be afraid of losing all their money? Those who allocated too much of their money into one stock.

Why would someone allocate too much of their money into one stock? Either because they do not have adequate insight to recognize buying opportunities, or because they are gamblers placing all their chips on red and hoping for a big, quick payout.

It is important that you do not invest more than 10% of your portfolio into one stock, no matter how attractive it looks. Time and time again you will be in a situation where one of your stocks unexpectedly plunges, and I guarantee you will make irrational decisions if you have a large percentage of your portfolio in this stock.

The simple act of diversifying your portfolio among different stocks allows you to remove nearly all fear from your decision-making, which is essential for getting rich in the market.

Why would someone panic buy? They fear missing out on a huge gain.

What kind of people would this be? Generally someone who has been on the sideline watching a stock waiting for the perfect buy-in opportunity, then the stock suddenly increases. Now the person feels that he is about to miss a perfect opportunity. Remember that there is no perfect buy-in opportunity.

There are also traders who panic buy only because others are panic buying. These people believe that the bandwagon is just starting up and they do not want to be left behind.

This herd-like mentality is prevalent in the market because most traders do not have the knowledge to understand when and why stocks should be bought and sold. They rely on the opinion of others, who are also just relying on the opinion of others.

This behavior explains why the Efficient Market Hypothesis is not called the Efficient Market Law. The notion that stock prices are perfectly efficient is just another hokey strategy derived from people overanalyzing things to the point of overlooking basic common sense.

31

The market is a chaotic place because it is full of fearful, greedy, ignorant people. These people all have very different personalities, agendas, and financial situations – all of which drive their investment decisions. For the Efficient Market Hypothesis to be true, investors would have to be robots in the same financial situation, all programmed to enter and exit stocks based on the exact same criteria.

The market is as diverse as the world population. This diversity means that the Efficient Market Hypothesis cannot even come close to being true.

Short-term stock prices resemble random dispersion across an unknown and changing baseline. This randomness effect is caused by millions of people participating together in the marketplace with their own specific needs and personalities.

Unless we personally knew each one of these people, it would be impossible to predict their actions – especially on a daily basis.

The core principle of becoming a billionaire

Is it beginning to be clear why I recommended selling after a 3% gain?

Let me give you a hint. The more you flip a coin, the more you will achieve a 50% split between heads and tails. Thus if you bet $100 million on heads and it lands heads – you got lucky once and stand at 100% success. If you kept betting, eventually you would trend towards a 50% success rate.

Although stock movements are not inherently random like a coin toss, they appear random to any one person because of the countless immeasurable variables that all exert a unique and continuously changing influence on each stock.

Nonetheless, if the market appears random then we should treat its movements as random. In the short-term, it is more probable that stock prices will randomly fluctuate up and down rather than constantly move in one direction. In the long-term, prices will trend upwards because certain stronger variables overshadow weaker variables.

This is similar to the scientific model used to predict the genetic makeup of offspring. The dark hair gene is dominant over the light hair gene, but that does not mean that dark and light haired parents will have all dark haired children; it means that *most* of their children will have dark hair.

There is one important difference regarding stock market variables. Market variables change their dominance depending on the timeframe observed.

Short-term prices are influenced by recent news and other people's behavior. These variables dominate the other variables affecting long-term prices, which is why the stock market continually fluctuates up and down in the short-term.

Long-term prices are influenced by company performance and the government's monetary and fiscal policies (namely inflation). These variables dominate the variables that affect short-term prices, which is why the stock market has always risen over the long-term.

I have devoted many hours to studying market movements, analyzing historical data, reading investment publications, and my personal favorite: meditation with the sole focus on how one could get rich in the stock market. Remember, any problem can be solved with insightful thinking, and here is what I have discovered.

Everyone agrees that the stock market will move up over the long-term, it just may take 20-30 years depending on the frequency and impact of bear markets.

What if there were no bear markets – what if the stock market were just one never-ending bull market? You would be rich. You would never lose the principal, but more importantly, the effect of compound interest would catapult your portfolio to an unimaginable amount.

Let us evaluate this statement with an example. For simplicity, assume there are 250 trading days per year and you start with a $100 thousand principal, each day making a compounded 0.5% gain on your principal.

After three years you would have earned 750 days of 0.5% compounded gains, and would now be toting a cool $4.19 million. See the chart below.

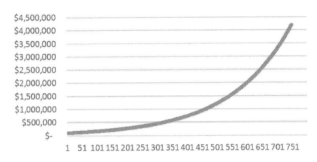

Compounding gains with no losses

Now assume the same situation, except you did not earn compound interest. You simply held on to a stock that earned 0.5% each day for three years. After three years you would only have <u>$374 thousand</u>. See the chart below.

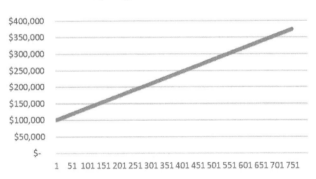

Simple gains with no losses

Big difference from $4.19 million. Comparing the two charts, you can visualize how much more money you earn when compounding your gains versus relying on simple gains.

How do you earn simple interest? Buy and hold a stock; the amount it appreciates after X years is your total gain.

How do you earn compound interest? Buy a stock when it is low, sell once you earn a small gain, and then buy a different stock with your bigger money supply.

In other words, sell your fish to buy a bigger net.

Each time that you sell stocks for small gains, you are increasing, or *realizing*, the amount of money available to invest into the next stock. On the other hand, if you hold a stock forever then you are never increasing the amount of money invested in it; your money supply does not grow until you sell the stock.

The simple interest chart is even more generous than how the market really moves. Think about it. The same stock will not continuously increase 0.5% every day, but every day there will be stocks that go up 0.5%.

Note the importance of this statement. You cannot earn consistent gains by holding a stock for the long-term. In fact, you earn consistent gains by *not* holding a stock for the long-term.

Now we finally come full circle back to the original concept of selling at a 3% gain. Since compounded interest has such a large effect on your portfolio, you will do yourself a colossal disservice by holding long-term. Long-term holding allows you to collect only simple interest, made upon inconsistent gains.

Some investors like to justify long-term investing because gains are taxed at lower rates. Stocks held under a year are taxed as ordinary income while stocks held over a year are taxed as capital gains (which are about 10-15% lower than ordinary rates). If these people are in a mood to stretch things, they will also point out that you pay less commission fees when holding long-term.

Let me get the second argument out of the way first because it is an easy one to disprove. If you remove $14 every day from the compounded example (assuming a $7 buy and $7 sell commission), you are left with $4.07 million after three years. I will gladly take that over the $374 thousand, thank you very much.

Regarding the tax rate, I agree taxes are a bummer and can put a beating on your compound interest, but you must remember that to pay the long-term capital gains rate of 15% you have to hold your stock over a year, which means no compound interest for at least a year. The 10-15% tax savings is trivial when compared to compounded interest gains.

Assume the worst-case scenario for a short-term investor; our investor is in the highest tax bracket from wages alone, which means she is taxed at a 39.6% ordinary income tax rate and a 20% long-term capital gains rate. Therefore all gains under a year will be taxed at 39.6% and all gains over a year will be taxed at 20%.

Starting with a hundred thousand dollars and investing only for the short-term, at the end of the third year she will have $1.53 million net profit, after taxes and commissions. If she would have held on to her stock for the long-term, selling after three years, then at a 20% tax rate she will have $299 thousand net profit.

As you can see, even considering taxes there is still a great difference between short-term and long-term holding.

In addition, would you really trust the market to value your stock fairly at the end of the year, considering the numerous variables that can exert influence?

No. You cannot trust the market to fairly value your stock at any time. It is very possible that you invest in an undervalued stock, it trends upward a few months, then it dips back down to the original value before the year is up. In essence, holding the stock all this time resulted in wasted gains that could have been made elsewhere.

Furthermore, it is unreasonable to assume that a single stock will remain the best investment opportunity for an entire year. If you invest in Company A because it appears 50% undervalued, are you confident that another stock will not show up later in the year that appears 70% undervalued?

Remember, there is no one perfect buy-in opportunity out there.

Then what opportunity is closest to being perfect? Let us do some insightful thinking here.

The perfect stock would be so predictable that every day you could buy at a 5% discount in the morning and then sell at a 5% premium in the afternoon. This way you could realize consistent, compounded gains.

So think to yourself – which stock most resembles this behavior?

The answer is not one particular stock, but rather *all* stocks in the market.

Stocks never move up in such a neat and clean fashion as shown in the second chart. If you hold onto the same stock for years, you are risking a long-term depressed price, or worse, being wiped out by a bankruptcy. No matter how strong you think the company is, you cannot predict its future. This is why long-term stock options are significantly more expensive than short-term options.

<u>No one stock will rise every day, however every day there will be stocks that rise.</u>

Then, the key to getting rich is not to hold the same stock for a long period, hoping it will rise. The key to getting rich is to buy whichever stock is going up for that particular day, then sell once it does go up.

Here is a real-world example if there are any skeptics left out there.

Below is a chart of the NASDAQ Composite for 1996 – 2013, taken from Yahoo! Finance. I chose the NASDAQ because an index has much less unsystematic risk than a single stock.

In other words, an individual stock will have its own unique factors that affect its stock price, factors that would not apply to other stocks. I want to remove these unique factors and show you an overall market view.

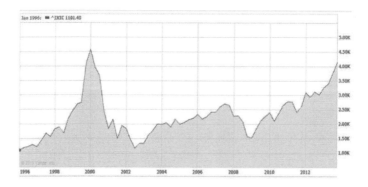

In 1996, the NASDAQ opened at 1101. Assume the investor purchased at this point and decided he was going to hold it forever. As of December 23, 2013 (the last day on this chart), the NASDAQ closed at 4148. That is a gain of 376% over the course of 18 years, or about 20% per year.

How much money would this equate to? Well, if you invested a hundred thousand dollars in 1996, 18 years later you would have $300,000 (considering 20% federal capital gains tax). Not exactly what I would call rich.

On the other hand, consider you decided not to endure the ups and downs of the NASDAQ. Instead you find a group of 10 undervalued stocks that are more likely to rise than fall. You invest ten thousand dollars in each of these 10 stocks for a total investment of $100 thousand.

You decide to sell a stock anytime it rises 3% over your cost basis. After selling, you immediately reinvest the proceeds into a different stock that you believe is undervalued at the time. You never sell a stock for a loss unless the company experiences some sort of extraordinary event, such as impending bankruptcy or probable fraud.

40

Assume that you are able to sell five (half) of your week at a 3% gain each. This means your entire portfolio value increased 1.5% per week.

After one year, your hundred thousand dollars would have increased to $170,000, assuming that you paid the highest federal tax rate of 40%. Now here is the kicker – after 18 years (the length of time you held the NASDAQ) your after-tax portfolio would have compounded to **$1.77 billion**.

That's right, you could have ended up with $370,000 holding the NASDAQ for 18 years, or you could have earned $1.77 billion by choosing not to sit idly through the ups and downs of the market.

Want another $1.77 billion? Just use the same strategy for another two years. That is the power of compound interest, and the way billionaires are created.

Well, all this is fine and dandy, but is it really possible to sell 5 stocks per week at a 3% gain each?

Absolutely. In fact, it is my routine. Test it out for yourself – pull the historical price data for 10 stocks and divide the week's high by the week's low. There is a very good chance most stocks are far above a 3% high/low (volatility) per week.

Let us try a more conservative approach and analyze something less volatile than a single stock, such as an Exchange Traded Fund (ETF) comprised of many stocks. I am going to test XLE, which is a highly traded Energy Select Sector ETF.

Running the weekly price data for this ETF, I see it averaged 5.6% volatility, per week, over a 10-year period. From another perspective, this ETF had at least a 3% volatility per week for 80% of the weeks over the past 10 years.

What does this mean? If a huge ETF such as XLE is volatile enough to trade a high-low range of least 3%, for 80% of the time, think of how volatile any single stock will trade. It is not only possible – it is probable – that you will be able to sell at least five stocks per week at a 3% gain each.

Remember, you are able to buy and sell the same stock multiple times per day (albeit in a margin account with at least $25,000 invested – thanks to our kind big brothers at the Securities and Exchange Commission).

It is normal to see a stock bounce up and down 3% multiple times per day. If three of your ten stocks bounce 3% twice in a day then you have already exceeded your quota of the 1.5% gain per week.

See how practical this is becoming? There is no guessing when you should sell a stock – you sell once it hits 3%, no questions asked.

So why should you sell at a 3% gain versus any other percentage?

When I first began researching the stock market, my strategy was to purchase undervalued stocks and hold until they became fairly valued. Each day I would watch my stocks move up and down, but never come close to hitting that subjective fair value mark.

I thought to myself, what is the use of holding onto an undervalued stock if no one else thinks it is undervalued? Sure, it may be a safe investment that will eventually pay off – but when will this happen? Will I still be holding this stock five years from now, waiting for the market to understand what a great buy it is?

Each day I watched my undervalued stocks, like ants, take two steps forward then one step back until I finally had enough; there had to be a smarter way to invest. So I opened Excel, downloaded the daily historical price data for my top 50 undervalued stocks, and set on a mission to find the sweet-spot – the percentage above cost basis that would yield the most gain.

Surprisingly, I found that 2.5 – 3.5% above cost basis yielded the largest overall gain, by far.

The higher you sell above cost basis, the more return you make on the sale; however, you sell less frequently.

The lower you sell above cost basis, the more frequently you are able to sell the stock; however, you earn less with each sale.

There was little difference in gains when selling between 2.5% and 3.5%; nevertheless 3% still showed the highest gain among all.

Keep in mind that every stock is different. One may trade within a 2% range while another trades within a 5% range.

These ranges are not set in stone, though. Just because one stock currently trades at 5% does not mean that it will always trade within that range. It would be a waste of time trying to identify each stock's trading range; doing so would be no different than speculators trying to justify a stock purchase on whichever rain dance they prefer to rely on.

You can get any outcome desired if you twist enough variables together. Instead of letting greed fool you into performing unnecessary complex and tedious analyses, it is most effective and efficient to keep things smart and simple.

This is why I prefer to stick with the general rule of selling 3% over cost basis, while giving preference to the more volatile stocks.

Volatility is an important characteristic when evaluating potential stock candidates, along with other fundamental factors that will be explained later. However, one thing I want to mention now about volatility is that you will never be able to perfectly time a stock's high and low.

Just because a stock trades at 5% volatility per week does not mean you will earn 5% on that stock. The 5% volatility only allows you to understand the stock's fluctuations relative to other stocks. You need to set smart entry points in order to increase the chance that upwards volatility will push your stock 3% over cost basis. Entry points will be discussed later.

Breaking the rules

You will often face the situation where you purchased a stock last week; it traded flat until this afternoon when it finally went up 2% over your cost basis. You are now up $200 on your original $10,000 investment. Should you sell now while you are ahead or wait for it to reach a 3% gain?

It depends. However, unlike others who enjoy giving this answer to get out of a tough question, I am actually going to give you practical insight here.

Most volatility occurs around the market open and the market close. There is a greater chance during these periods that one of your stocks will exceed 3%. The same applies to buy-in points. Stocks are usually oversold at the market open or close, which make great buy-in opportunities for you.

So, in the morning if I see that one of my stocks is up 2%, I may sell it if the stock has been trading flat for a while (meaning it has a high likelihood of dipping back down due to investors eager to make a profit and get out).

I also may sell if there is a much better opportunity out there. For example, if a strong, undervalued stock randomly sinks 5% in the morning then I may sell one of my other stocks for a 2% gain. Doing so allows me to collect a sure gain while entering another stock at a very attractive price.

So yes, it is okay to sell a stock for less than 3% if you have a good reason to do so. A good reason. Not that you were just itching to click a button.

Although you may sell a little lower than 3% to take advantage of a particular opportunity, you should never sell for a loss unless some extraordinary event happened to the company that significantly changes its outlook (bankruptcy, impending financial troubles, fraud).

You will constantly feel pressure to exit non-performing positions at a loss, just to feel the relief of exiting out of a losing position and entering into a better opportunity.

Most traders give into this feeling, which is why most traders are unsuccessful. The average trader enters a position after a recent price increase, and exits the same position after a recent decrease.

This kind of behavior is the opposite of a successful trading strategy. No matter how gloomy things appear – the strong, undervalued stocks eventually will go back up. And no matter how optimistic things appear, all stocks will eventually dip down.

To be successful you need to control your fear by entering and holding positions that are down, and control your greed by exiting positions that are up.

Stated again – to become rich you need to act as an outsider peering in to the market, using its fluctuations and irrationality to your advantage, rather than the majority of investors who let the market control them. Control your own emotions and profit from those who cannot.

Where most people go wrong

Now that you understand the massive difference between long-term and short-term trading, why doesn't everyone trade for the short-term?

First, there is a stigma about short-term trading thanks to the speculative traders out there. Speculative trading is purchasing a stock for its potential performance rather than its actual performance.

Penny stock trading is an example of speculative trading. The reason why these stocks are worth only pennies is because their underlying companies have little tangible worth and profit generation; most of them actually lose money each quarter and owe more than they own.

These stocks are prime targets for speculative traders, who, in my opinion, are gamblers more so than traders. The gamblers believe that since the price is so low, if they can buy 5 million shares for $0.0005 each ($2500 total), the price just has to spike up to $1 for their $2500 investment to increase to $5 million.

Great, so what is the chance of this happening? Well, $0.0005 to $1 is a <u>two-hundred thousand percent</u> gain. Yes, 200,000%.

What stock does that? None.

Then why do people think it can happen? Because they do not think in terms of percentages; they think in terms of dollars. These people see Google's stock price move $20 in one day and believe that their little penny stock can also move $20 in one day.

Inevitably, these companies declare bankruptcy and the gamblers lose their money. But every day, just like clockwork, people bet their hard-earned money that some sort of miracle will happen to their portfolios.

This behavior stems from greed; speculators want to get rich overnight with no effort. They do not have the patience to invest over a longer timeframe, nor the knowledge to understand that patience is a better investment strategy, nor the motivation to obtain this knowledge, nor the intelligence that they could be rich if they were motivated.

Another reason people do not trade for the short-term is because they do not have a methodology to quickly choose entry and exit points.

Most people have a very rudimentary stock selection methodology because they do not know how to evaluate a company's potential. They close their eyes, think about a well-known company, then buy into a position at the current market price.

A small portion of these people may look at the long-term stock chart or consider the company's viability, but that is usually the extent of their research.

People who limit their potential investment pools to such tight extremes will inevitably hold stocks for too long; they do not want to let go of a stock because they do not know which stock to replace it with. There are only so many well-known companies they can think of.

If you understand everything discussed so far then you are already ahead of many traders out there, but how do you reach that top percentile who end up striking it rich? You need a sound methodology to quickly choose stock entry and exit points. Doing so requires an understanding of market psychology and business fundamentals. This will be covered next.

To conclude this section, I bring you back to the original statement that people should not hold long-term if they have the ability to short-term trade.

The overall market will move up in the long-term but it will be riddled with many peaks and valleys. If your money just sits there, it will also be riddled with peaks and valleys (earning simple interest, I may add).

If you purchased the NASDAQ index in 1996, after subsequent the peaks and valleys your money would have been worth almost the same six years later in 2002. Then, another six years later in 2008, your money would still have been worth about the same.

Casual investors freak out when they see their nest egg has not grown in 12 years. They liquidate their investments at extreme lows and place the money in a certificate of deposit (CD) at a laughably low interest rate. Who is laughing about the interest rate? The bank, who then loans or invests this money back out for a laughably high interest rate.

One man's trash is another's treasure. The casual investor's panicky low sells are just your routinely calm buys. You did not experience the feeling of your portfolio dropping back down to its starting value because you have not hung around long enough in one stock to see it happen. You just see a very undervalued stock that will likely increase a quick 3%.

The market is setting record highs as I write this book. No one knows for sure how long it will sustain these prices, but I can assure you that there will be a substantial dip in the near future.

This could happen in the next few months or in the next couple of years, but it will come and it will bring everyone's portfolios down to shockingly low values. Fear and panic will spread throughout the market; people will ask the same question that is asked during every recession – is this the end of the stock market?

This nervousness will continue until everyone has a chance to calm down and realize that the world is not ending.

While everyone is losing days off their lives from stress, you are happily taking 3% gains – which interestingly are easiest to come by during widespread panic because the market is so volatile from many speculative investors selling and many value investors buying (take a look at the market's volatility during the late 2008 crash). It does not matter if the overall market trends downward over a few months. What matters is that there are widespread differences in opinion on the market's direction, and people are backing up their opinions with enormous trading volume.

Knowing that history will continue repeating yourself, you, as an insightful investor, will choose not to experience the peaks and valleys of long-term trading. Instead you will treat the market as a boxing match. Stick and move.

The reason boxers like Muhammad Ali, or more recently, Floyd Mayweather Jr., are so successful is not because they stand in front of their opponent and slug it out. They have such long and successful careers because they focus on <u>avoiding</u> beat downs by quickly popping their opponent then backing off before he has a chance to counterpunch.

Your market strategy should be the same way. Quickly pop into a strong company, take a small gain, and get out before the company or overall market knock you out with a haymaker out of nowhere.

Here is an interesting tidbit for you. Nearly half of the market's losses occur between yesterday's closing price and today's opening price. This means that you can avoid almost half of the market's downturns by not holding stocks between days.

Do not misunderstand me, though; it is still better to hold stocks overnight than to sell at a loss before the market close. However if given the chance, you should aim to hold stocks for as little time as possible.

Pretend you are a cowboy showing up to a desert town. Hang around the town long enough to grab the bank's money bag then get the hell out of Dodge before the sheriff catches you. Move on to the next town and repeat.

To sum it up – stocks are dating, but not marriage material.

Part III – Make your momma proud: Choosing the right stocks

Don't be the one who, after sobering up, regrets getting into a relationship with that awful person. Let one of the other drunks get stuck with him or her.

Flaws behind technical and fundamental analysis

The stock market is remarkably similar to late night bar hookups; peer pressure and irrational thinking are rampant in both. A group of friends with a lot to drink can influence each other to do things they never would do otherwise.

Likewise, a group of traders, drunk on greed and fear, can influence each other to buy stocks at unreasonably high prices and sell at ridiculously low prices.

You can profit against their irrationality by not getting caught up in this greed and fear. To do so you need a smart strategy to identify stock opportunities, and then to identify entry and exit points.

There are many schools of thought on stock selection. Generally all strategies are derived on one or both of the following methodologies: *technical analysis* and *fundamental analysis*.

Technical analysis involves searching for stocks that have exhibited a particular chart pattern, leading the technical trader to believe that the price will move a certain direction.

A single stock chart can exhibit dozens of patterns per week, all of which may quickly change the trader's outlook on the stock. Consequently, technical traders prefer short-term trading.

Pure technical analysis is the weaker of the two methodologies. Just think of how many successful technical traders you can name versus fundamental traders. I will go even further by saying that technical analysis is so popular because of *hindsight bias* and laziness.

Humans, with their intense desire to rationalize the world around them, naturally suffer from hindsight bias. This occurs when one falsely believes, after a completed event, that he correctly predicted the outcome before the event even started. In other words, people overestimate their ability to predict future events.

The hindsight bias can be observed in elections. Two weeks prior to the presidential election, voters are asked to predict a winning candidate. Naturally these opinions are split approximately 50/50 between the Republican and Democratic candidates.

After the election, the same people are asked who they predicted would win the race. If the Republican won, then the majority of people will think they had predicted the Republican winner all along, and vice-versa.

Technical traders spend time trying to identify stock chart patterns, then relying on these patterns to predict price movements. Before the market opens, a trader may look at 30 different company charts and form opinions on how each will move during the day. The trader may change his opinion five times on a single stock before settling on a final decision. At the end of the day, whether the stock moved up 5% or down 5%, he will still believe that he predicted that outcome all along.

As illogical as this sounds, the trader is actually correct. His first opinion may have been that the stock was going to increase 5%; he just later changed his mind and concluded it would decrease 5%. At the end of the day he will, either consciously or unconsciously, brush off whichever was the wrong prediction.

No harm done, right? False, there is harm done. After reassuring himself of his Superman-like technical analysis ability, he will begin having more confidence in his predictions. With more confidence comes more unnecessary risk-taking, and eventual losses.

Some people suffer from hindsight bias more than others. You know someone who believes he is always right in every situation. Even when faced with contrary facts, he makes excuses that some external force caused him to be wrong, or even outright deny that he ever made the incorrect statements.

The more one suffers from hindsight bias, the less successful he will be – both in stocks and in life. If one believes that he is always right, then there is no need to change. If there is no need to change, no progress is ever made.

The hindsight bias occurs more often in technical analysis for two reasons: it is visual and it can be manipulated to one's liking.

Humans are naturally visual creatures and are more likely to explain past events and predict future events when presented with pictures (think of how management likes to understand and explain results using colorful charts and graphs).

Humans are prone to believing and even liking things they can easily understand. If you want to win someone over, simply be understandable to that person.

Recognize that being understandable is different than being predictable. If you are overly predictable then you will be perceived as boring.

An understandable person is a relatable person. This means you are able to communicate your life experiences, struggles, and dreams through your personality – without a specific mention of them. This encourages people to *want to* help you, without ever asking for it.

Remember that every action a person takes in life is solely for his or her benefit. Therefore winning people to your cause means they actually feel good about helping achieve your goals.

It takes a very rare and effective personality to win people over in this fashion, which explains why so very few people are able to achieve this feat. For people to care about your goals, you must care about their goals even more. For people to respect you, you need to respect them even more. They need to believe that they will benefit themselves by helping you.

Considering that humans have an inherent attraction towards understandable things, do you see why technical analysis is so popular? A stock chart with shifting lines and pretty colors is easier to understand than a bunch of numbers and formulas.

The other reason why the hindsight bias is more prevalent in technical analysis is because it can be manipulated to fit any situation. Technical analysis uses many more variables than fundamental analysis; there are thousands of ways that indicators can be combined to conveniently fit a past event.

Remember, humans have an innate desire to explain the world around them and will attempt to do so even if it means using illogical rationale. After an hour of studying a chart, clicking various indicators on and off, the technical trader can conclude that eight different indicators were responsible for the 5% gain. Going forward, he uses these eight indicators to predict future movements and finds that his secret formula does not seem to work as expected. Oh well, must be the market's problem.

Laziness also contributes to the popularity of technical analysis. Ponder this question for a second. What is the difference between an armchair quarterback and Drew Brees?

Drew Brees has spent an enormous amount of the time and energy to learn the quarterback position. Doing so has ingrained certain reflexes into his psyche, whereby if X happens then he should perform Y to achieve the best outcome.

In contrast, the armchair quarterback prefers to tell his buddies what the real quarterback should be doing. This makes him feel intelligent and important. He wants the prestige of Brees without putting in the effort to obtain it. No one thinks the armchair quarterback is a prestigious player (other than maybe the armchair receiver and running back sitting next to him).

It is much easier to quarterback a game from your chair than it is on an NFL field, which is why 99.999872% of Americans perform quarterbacking duties in their own home (yes, I actually did the math).

Technical analysis is the armchair quarterback equivalent of stock evaluations. People do not want to put in the time and energy required to learn business fundamentals; they would rather stare at charts for hours and believe they can predict the future.

I am not saying that fundamental analysts are supreme beings compared to technical analysts, far from it. I am saying that too many technical traders have lost sight of the basic stock market concept, where one trades his money for a share in the company's net assets and future profits.

People get caught up in their overly complex analyses, patterns, and hype which causes them to lose focus of the big picture. Over the long-term, the market still behaves according to basic business principles. Therefore you want to invest according to these principles, not according to chart patterns which are largely affected by hype.

Hype does not live forever; massively overpriced stocks will eventually crash and extremely undervalued stocks will eventually rise.

Pure technical analysis disregards such factors and instead tries to rely on chart movements; much how a fortuneteller relies on tealeaf patterns to predict your life. As I mentioned before, how many rich technical traders do you know? I would predict that you know the same amount of rich gamblers as you do rich technical traders.

On the other side of the coin is fundamental analysis. This involves searching for stocks that have certain attributes or stocks trading at certain ratios. These factors help the fundamental trader understand if the stock is over or undervalued.

Fundamental trading involves finding companies that are supposedly mispriced – which can take weeks, months, or even years for the stock price to correct itself. Therefore, fundamental traders usually prefer investing for the long-term.

Fundamental analysis is the safer of the two. If you enter a stock position because a company appears undervalued,

even if the price drops you are able to ho
without worrying about losing all your money

Compare this situation to technical trading. If you enter a position based solely on chart patterns and then the price suddenly drops, you cannot be confident that the stock will ever recover. You will likely either sell the stock out of fear and take a quick loss, or hold onto it for a while and take a larger loss.

Trading ranges

Technical analysis totes one advantage over fundamental analysis. It attempts to apply psychological elements to the market, some of which are valid techniques.

For example, the terms *resistance* and *support* are basic technical concepts. Technical traders believe that stocks trade within a range; the high point of the range called resistance and the low point called support. While it is possible that a stock can cross either end of the range, this situation is unlikely and usually requires some sort of news to push the price out of its trading range.

Trading ranges are true and real. A $10 stock that once traded at $30 is perceived to be more undervalued than a $20 stock that once traded at $30. This perception applies even if the $20 stock has better fundamentals than the $10 stock.

People place undue importance on a stock's historical price. They believe that if a stock previously traded at $30 then there is a chance it could reach those levels again. The opposite perception occurs when a stock is trading higher now than in the past. People believe it has a greater chance of dropping down to those lower levels.

This phenomenon is the reason why similar companies can trade at vastly different P/B and P/E ratios. Additionally, this is the primary drawback of fundamental investing.

Fundamental investing assumes that stock prices will always follow company fundamentals. While it is true that most stock prices will eventually correct themselves to better reflect company fundamentals, the irrational market can make you wait a long time before seeing this happen. Hence, you will earn a decent return through long-term fundamental investing, however you can earn a much higher return by using the market's random price fluctuations to your advantage; hedged by the fact that you are holding a fundamentally undervalued company with the likelihood to increase over the long-term.

We can conclude that trading ranges are real, even if they are built on irrational thinking. We know that a stock's trading range is primarily based on its historical trading range – but what is its historical trading range based on? You cannot have a chicken without an egg. There has to be some factor that provides an overall influence and direction to a stock's trading range, right?

Correct. The influencing factor is each trader's cost basis within the stock. For example, if 70% of stockholders bought in at $13 then they will be hesitant to sell the stock below this price, and $13 will appear as a support level. If the stock spikes up to $20, many of these traders will sell to realize a substantial gain. The sell-off will be particularly quick if the traders have held onto the stock for a while, or if the company is financially weak and does not appear to have a prosperous future. Either way, $20 will appear to be a resistance level because many people decided to sell at that particular time.

These are sound theories, however many people still do not utilize them correctly. For instance, assume the previously mentioned stock hit a low of $13 twice in a week, then bounced back up to the normal trading range of $14.

Technical traders may consider $13 to be a support point when looking at the weekly trading range. However, what if the stock traded at a low of $11 just a month earlier, and a low of $8 a year ago? These are all points that could be considered support levels.

Therefore we can say that support and resistance levels are derived from two factors: 1) Traders' personalities; and 2) Timeframe that the stock traded within that range.

Most stock charts are drawn in specific periods such as 3 months, 6 months, 1 year, etc.

If 366 days ago the stock's low was $8, then two days later (364 days ago) it reached $11, traders looking at a 2-year chart will believe the low to be $8 while traders looking at a 1-year chart will believe the low to be $11.

You can see how such a small variable influences trader decisions. Consider how their decisions would be different if the $8 low fell within the 1-year chart rather than the 2-year chart. More investors would believe $8 to be the low, and more would believe the stock was overpriced at $13.

There is a lot of subjective opinion that goes into technical analysis, which is why I recommend only using a few specific technical concepts to support a primarily fundamental analysis.

For my personal portfolio, I do not attempt to derive support and resistance levels by looking at a chart. Instead, I estimate the cost basis of all shareholders in a particular stock by dividing the number of shares traded at each price range by the total shares outstanding. I perform this calculation on about a year of historical price data.

Sometimes 100% of the outstanding shares were traded in the past recent week, whereas in others only 50% of the outstanding shares were traded in the past year.

You can be more confident in a stock's support and resistance levels if a large percentage of total shares were traded within a short period. This is because you have better certainty of everyone's cost basis.

If 100% of a company's outstanding shares were traded within a month, you would be relatively confident that most of the shareholders have a cost basis somewhere within the last month's price range.

Be aware that this does not mean that all shareholders bought in during the past month; some shares could have been traded five times among the same group of people within the past month. Thus 100% of the total number of shares may have been traded, but it does not mean that each individual share was traded within the past month.

If a stock trades infrequently then you may need to analyze years of price data to estimate everyone's cost basis. To add to the complexity, generally the longer a shareholder has held the stock the more eager he is to get rid of it – people want money quick and easy. When a company has shareholders with such a diverse range of holding times, from years to days, it is difficult to predict their cost bases.

Anyhow, there are many other strategies involved in technical and fundamental analysis that I will not go into. First, because there are many books already out there on this subject; and second, because I believe many of the strategies are unnecessarily complex and worthless. These strategies often turn into *self-fulfilling prophecies*, meaning that investors falsely convince themselves that they have the best strategy out there.

Hence, I will cover technical and fundamental analysis only to the extent that I believe their usefulness in evaluating trading opportunities.

The fallibility of support and resistance levels

We said that support and resistance levels are real. The problem is that they are based on irrationalities rather than fundamentals. Irrationalities in support and resistance levels, like all irrationalities in the market, predict stock prices only for an indefinite amount of time.

So a technical trader's model could work as long as a year or as short as an hour. This uncertainty is what gets them into trouble, causing them to nervously stare at charts all day with their hands on top of their head.

Basing your entry and exit points solely on support and resistance levels is like playing Russian roulette – you may be correct the first few times, but eventually you will lose.

Every trader has their own entry/exit points. Some consciously plan when they will enter and exit; others act on a whim. Any way you look at it, entry/exit points are based on so many personal decisions and are constantly changing. We cannot expect to predict other's actions with any real significance.

So what are technical traders left with then? Are support and resistance levels useless?

It depends what you consider useless. Consider what happens when two thousand technical traders look at the same chart, all seeing the same two bounces off a $13 low. The "ah-hah" light bulb collectively goes off and a stronger $13 support level is created.

It is possible that the majority of traders are actually in at an $11 cost basis and the $13 support level has no real backing. That does not matter, though. People routinely purchase stocks in companies that have no assets, no earnings, no backing at all.

So the facts actually do not matter in this situation. All that matters is that people *believe* that these are the facts; belief is all that is needed to create support and resistance levels.

Thus we can conclude that support and resistance levels are not useless. However they are often derived from the mere observation that the stock price happened to bounce off a certain threshold.

In actuality the $13 support level could have been created by a millionaire in New York, who had happened to sit down at his computer at the moment when the stock hit $13. He thought to himself, "Great buying opportunity" and proceeded to buy a chunk of shares, forcing the price back up to $13.20. Others saw the spike and, fearful of missing out on the party train, all bought in and forced the stock back up to $14.

A few weeks later the millionaire sells his shares, causing a trend back down to $13. The technical traders look back at the historical chart and observe that a few weeks ago the stock dropped to the $13 "support level" and quickly rebounded up. They all buy in at $13, thinking that the price has to go up from here, and the cycle repeats itself. The more this cycle runs, the more that this support level is reinforced.

Notice the millionaire is not participating in the stock anymore, but his one-time action of buying a chunk of shares at $13 started this whole cycle of support at $13 and resistance at $14.

Think about the old black-and-white slapstick comedies where a troublemaker lobs a pie at an unsuspecting bystander. The bystander mistakes the culprit for an innocent bystander, and throws a pie at that guy. This cycle repeats itself, starting a crazed food fight with pies flung in every direction as the troublemaker tiptoes out of the room. In the end, everyone in the room is left in a mess of strawberry filling and whipped cream, while the spotless troublemaker is at home reclining back in his chair with a devious smirk on his face.

You do not want to get caught up in stock market pie fights. You do not know when they will start and end, nor do you know how messy things will get.

One of the participants may pull out a knife and stab his rival. This causes another to pull a gun and shoot his rival. Soon guns are blazing and bodies are left strewn across the dining hall. One simple pie toss resulted in twenty casualties.

In market terminology, a slightly negative earnings report for a speculative company results in a price crash. If this happens to be a well-known company, its crash reverberates throughout the industry and may cause an industry-wide crash.

Market crashes are burned into the public's consciousness, which is why most people believe stock investing to be so risky. There are horror stories of people's life savings being wiped out in less than a day from a market crash. However, realize that on the other side of the horror stories are lucky traders who just made a ton of cash.

Notice I did not refer to these people as "insightful investors," but as lucky traders. No insightful investor would put his portfolio at such great risks by investing in these over-priced, over-hyped companies. My objective is to show you how to be an insightful investor who gets rich in the market, not to be the one that makes someone else rich.

To be insightful you must understand the psychology that initiates and feeds market crashes, with the objective of removing yourself from the madness before it even begins.

Psychology of market crashes

"Bagholder" is a term thrown around in the investment community to describe a person that is left holding a worthless stock after the hype has died down. The idea is that when a stock is popular, the "bag" frequently changes hands from one to the other, each time trading at a higher and higher price. The underlying company, or bag, has no tangible value. The only reason it is in such demand is, ironically, because it is in such demand.

This concept frequently occurs in society. Consider the city of Dubai within the United Arab Emirates. It is an economically strong city in the Middle East only because it is a popular tourist attraction; and it is a popular tourist attraction because it is an economically strong city in the Middle East. It has little oil reserves or other tangible value. It even had to be "bailed out" by Abu Dhabi, the UAE capital, because of excessive infrastructure spending combined with declining tourist interest. At this rate, I would not be surprised if the city implodes over the next decade because it has no real value to it.

Another example, consider attraction between humans, particularly women's attraction to males. The more "in-demand" a male is, the more attractive he appears to women. Since he appears more attractive, he is more in-demand.

George Soros, the famous hedge fund manager, explained this concept in his book *The Alchemy of Finance* (although he did so using such dull and long-winded terminology that would put the normal reader to sleep within five minutes; I already summarized it with a more relatable analogy so thankfully you can skip that tedious read). He basically argued that future price movements are influenced by public perception, and vice-versa.

So yes, this behavior rears its ugly head in the stock market. Traders often buy overpriced stocks only because they believe that someone else will want the stock soon, and for a higher price.

This game can, and frequently does, continue for a while until the stock falls out of favor. Then all of a sudden no one wants to pay higher prices for the stock because people stop believing that others will want it. This starts a snowball effect, where more people now believe that others do not want the stock. The sudden drop in demand quickly pushes the stock price back down to its true value, taking a huge bite from those unlucky fools who last purchased the stock.

Take for example one of the famous search engines of the 90s – InfoSpace, which is now known as Blucora (InfoSpace sounded much better).

See the Yahoo! Finance chart for InfoSpace below.

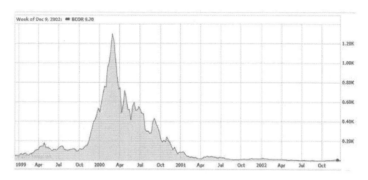

InfoSpace was another casualty of the dot-com crash. Notice the huge price spike in November 1999 that peaked in February 2000. In this period, the stock price increased from $155/share to $1300/share, a gain of over 800% in four months.

Logically, it is very unlikely that a semi-established company can increase its actual value this much in four months. While InfoSpace's revenues did increase three-fold in this period, their cost of revenue and operating expenses grew nearly as much; thus they still were losing millions of dollars per quarter while the stock price kept climbing.

InfoSpace's stock surge was primarily due to herd mentality. Speculative traders were willing to pay higher and higher prices for a company that was not increasing its actual value. Other traders saw a consistent uptrend and did not want to miss out on the party train, so they began paying outrageous prices for the stock. This snowballed to a point where no one wanted to buy the stock at these prices anymore. The shareholders realized they were holding overpriced stock that may be worthless soon. Fear set in and caused a downward slide.

You can avoid getting caught up in these situations by choosing strong, undervalued stocks.

Essential attributes of a strong stock

The core strategy of stock selection is finding a company that you would feel comfortable holding in the long-term if the market goes sour. Recall in Part II, I described how active short-term trading is much more profitable than passive long-term investing.

Your strategy should be to sell as soon as you hit a 3% gain; however, you are not always guaranteed to get a quick 3% gain. There is always the chance that the stock, or even the overall market, crashes after you enter a position. When this happens you do not want to be holding a stock for a debt-riddled startup company trying to figure out time-travel.

During panic phases, investors take their money out of speculative stocks and place them in safer investments; usually companies with tangible value and consistent profits. Speculative stock prices go down and undervalued stock prices go up. This is known as a market correction and is what value (fundamental) investors live for.

Before entering a position, you need to determine if the stock could reasonably survive a turn for the worse. This means a company that currently earns a good return on assets/equity, is not overpriced (underpriced is ideal), is becoming financially stronger over the years, has enough liquid assets to pay its bills, and fits in with your diversification strategy. Once a prospect is found, an entry point must be determined based on the stock's recent price performance and its price volatility.

Keep in mind that when evaluating these factors, it is important to consider the company's industry. One company may look underpriced when compared to market averages; however, it may actually be the most overvalued company in that industry.

Other less important, but still helpful factors to consider are: if the stock is at a long-term peak or valley, the percentage of shares shorted, the percentage of shares owned by insiders/institutions, the dividend yield (if applicable), cash flow, investor sentiment, and management's character.

I will give my recommendations for each one of these factors in detail, assuming you have a basic understanding of how these ratios work. The scope of this book is not to explain the basics of financial metrics. This has been covered to death in many books (and most books actually stop at the basics because of the author's fear/laziness/ignorance to provide valuable, insightful information). Therefore to go into this again would be a waste of our time. An Internet search will prove useful if you need to understand the basics of these ratios.

Return on assets/equity: The first thing I look at is a stock's return on assets and equity because it shows how well management is working with what they have, and what could they do if they had more of it. If both of these are negative, I disregard the stock. If both of these are under 5%, I disregard the stock. If both of these are low compared to industry average, I disregard the stock.

Plenty of companies make money, so there is no reason to invest in one that is not making money. Investing with the notion that the company could eventually become profitable is a form of speculation. This is something an insightful investor does not need to do.

If you find that the company is profitable, then great, it passed the initial cut. You then need to assess how much money it is making relative to its industry.

You can generally expect that Internet companies with little capital assets will earn a higher ROA than a mining company with a large amount of capital assets. This does not mean the Internet company is a better ran company; it just operates a different type of business.

However if you noticed that an Internet-based website development company had a 40% ROE compared to another with a 20% ROE, then the former may be a better ran company. There is no guarantee, but a company that leads its industry in ROA or ROE is a good start for investment decisions.

Keep in mind that a company can be on top of its industry and still have a negative ROA/ROE. This is a clear sign of a speculative industry. If the industry leader cannot even make a profit, then stay away from the industry.

Only speculative traders hope to get lucky. We do not hope to get lucky; we actually try to remove the luck factor because it is always possible that luck will favor the other trader.

Of course, there will be some companies with awful ROAs/ROEs that eventually become profitable, but why would you want to risk finding these exceptions when there are plenty of good companies out there? Would you marry a widowed serial killer in hopes that she will later change her ways?

Over or underpriced: After finding a company that is making money, you want to ensure its stock is not overpriced. There is no use investing in a profitable company if you pay 10 times over its worth (think back to the InfoSpace example).

I use three ratios to help determine if a stock is over or underpriced: P/B, P/Cash, and P/E.

P/B is most important because it is a direct measure of the company's tangible worth. Some people (gamblers) have no hesitation buying a stock that is trading over a 10 P/B ratio.

Think about it. Buying a 10 P/B ratio stock is literally trading $1 for $0.10 in return. Why would anyone do this?

It is because they are speculating, hoping that they can unload the stock before it corrects itself. Or maybe they just do not have business acumen. Either way, there are plenty of companies out there with low P/B ratios. The market always corrects itself, and when it does, it makes poor fools out of those who gave their money away for less in return.

Try to stick with companies trading at less than 1 P/B, meaning you are trading $1 for $1+ in company value. This is a smart strategy because if the company is ever acquired then you have a much greater chance of realizing a premium on your investment.

Undervalued companies are prime acquisition targets. If a company spends $10 million to buy another company with $30 million in net tangible assets, then it instantly earned 300% on its investment. If the acquired company was previously trading at $8 million, then its shareholders received a 25% premium over their investment. It is a win-win for both parties.

I have witnessed many undervalued companies get acquired for a substantial premium over its share price. By contrast, shareholders of an overvalued company will receive less premium during an acquisition than the shareholders of an undervalued company. Of course this is contingent on the overvalued company being offered a buyout. Many companies will not even attempt to purchase an overvalued company. They know that the shareholders will only approve a buyout if they receive a substantial premium over the current share price, so the cost/benefit is just not worth it.

With all this discussion on acquisitions, it is important to remember that you are not purchasing undervalued companies hoping for a buyout; you are purchasing them hoping for a 3% gain. If you happen to be holding it when a buyout is offered, all the better for you.

After a buyout announcement, the stock price will rise close to the buyout price. As the buyout becomes more certain, the stock price begins trending even closer to the buyout price.

There have been times when stocks trade about 10% lower than the buyout value, even when the buyout was only days away. These are great opportunities for a quick and certain gain. If the buyout is approved then you receive a swift 10%. At worse, if the buyout is rejected you are still left with an undervalued stock that the shareholders believe is worth more than the acquisition offering. Either way you are in a good position.

There is always the risk that one of your companies declares bankruptcy. Of course, the chance of this happening to one of your stocks should be nearly non-existent because you bought an undervalued company according to the principles outlined in this book. But still, the risk is always there.

Common shareholders are the last ones paid during a bankruptcy – after secured creditors, unsecured creditors, and preferred shareholders. Therefore it is better to be holding an undervalued company declaring bankruptcy than an overvalued company declaring bankruptcy.

If your company is trading at 1 P/B, then that means each share is worth the exact price of net tangible assets. Once these tangible assets are liquidated and everyone is paid off, there is a good chance you can receive a reasonable portion of your investment back. At best, you can receive 100% of your investment back.

On the other hand, if your company is trading at 5 P/B, then that means each share is trading five times over net tangible asset value. At best, you can expect to receive 20% of your investment back.

P/Cash is second in importance. Amazingly, some companies trade at lower prices than the amount of cash they have on-hand. Investing in a company with a 0.5 P/Cash ratio means that you can pay $1 per share that is immediately worth $2 in cold, hard cash. It is akin to going to the store and exchanging a one-hundred dollar bill for 10 twenty-dollar bills. These are often no-brainer investments; while other people are paying upwards of $20 for a $1 in cash (20 P/Cash ratio), you can be creating instant wealth for yourself.

As I write these words, most of the companies trading at low P/Cash ratios are Chinese companies. Many people are fearful of investing in Chinese companies because they do not place much trust in the accuracy of their financial statements. While there is never a guarantee that any company's financial statements are accurate, I am generally confident in a company's stated cash balances.

As an internal auditor by profession, I know that it is nearly impossible to overstate cash balances. Remember, all publicly traded companies must be independently audited by an external audit firm.

Cash is the easiest asset for external auditors to verify existence and value. Standard practice is to directly verify cash balances with the banks; so if it is there, it is there. Most investors do not know or understand how an external auditor performs their job, thus is an easy opportunity for you to benefit from their ignorance.

P/E is the third most useful valuation ratio, although it is the first most popular ratio. Investors place either too much or too little emphasis on P/E.

Speculators are the ones that place too little emphasis on P/E. A company could be trading at a 100 P/E level, with no signs of improvement, and people will still buy the stock. Businesswise this makes no sense. Would you ever buy a company where it would take 100 years to make a return on your investment?

It turns my stomach when people gamble their money away on these types of companies; however the feeling is bittersweet. If these gamblers would not be in the market then it would be a lot harder to choose undervalued stocks. So we can thank the gamblers for helping us get rich.

On the other end of the spectrum, some people make their sole decision based on P/E. If the P/E is too high, they totally disregard the stock when in actuality it could be an undervalued company that happened to have an off year.

P/E ratios are more volatile than some other ratios, such as P/B. If a company has an off year for whatever reason (and there are unavoidable off years), then its P/E ratio may be high while the P/B signifies that it is actually undervalued.

Having said that, I only invest in a high P/E company if the high P/E is due to some event outside the company's control. If it is in the middle of a product transition, that is fine. However if the company never turned a profit and is not expected to, then stay away from those.

When I refer to a high P/E company, I am referring to one with P/E over 20. I usually disregard anything over this point. There are plenty of pretty girls out there – why would I pick a chubby one then hope she goes on a diet?

Nearly every stock will fall during a crash; however, high P/E companies will fall harder and faster than undervalued companies will.

By the way, one word of advice – never invest in a stock just because it has a high P/E, as "growth investors" are known for.

It is amazing that some people believe it is a wise decision to invest in a stock specifically because it is overpriced. This is one of the most ridiculous ideas going around in the investment community. In effect, they are assuming that the stock price will rise only because it has risen in the past.

If this hypothesis was correct, then high P/E stocks will continue rising to infinity while low P/E stocks will fall to zero. The opposite is actually true. When a market correction occurs, traders flee speculative positions to find safe haven in value stocks; this brings high P/E stocks down and low P/E stocks up.

One other thing about P/E. If a company has negative earnings (thus no P/E), then I calculate P/E myself by dividing price by the negative earnings per share. Then multiply this result by 2 in order to inflate the negative P/E ratio, since I would rather invest in an overpriced company that actually earns money than a slightly less overpriced company that loses money (not that I recommend investing in an overpriced company at all).

Likewise, I would rather invest in a company with no P/E that is only $1 thousand away from profitability than a profitable company trading at a 100 P/E.

Earnings/asset growth: When evaluating a company's value, you want to assess its earnings and net asset growths over the past few years. Investors absolutely love companies that have a history of consistently increasing earnings because it suggests that the company is still a healthy, growing lad.

They also love (just maybe a tad less) when companies have a history of consistently increasing net tangible assets. This means the company is becoming financially stronger by increasing assets (cash, investments, property plant and equipment, etc.) faster than it is increasing liabilities (incurring debt). In other words, management is not partying the company's earnings away on booze and drugs. A more politically accepted statement is that shareholder equity is growing.

So if you know that investors love consistently increasing earnings and assets, what happens when a consistent company misses projected earnings for a quarter? Share price takes a poop. A poop is a great buy-in time for you, as long as the poop is due to irrational investor decisions

(OMG that number looks low!) and not a fundamental weakness in the company (such as an Apple supplier who loses the Apple account, which consisted of 95% of their total sales).

To give you a real-world example, a stock recently showed up on my radar as being very undervalued and having a huge price dip. Upon investigation I found out that this company reported lower earnings because they were in the middle of a product transition with their customers. This caused the stock to lose 30% of its value in one day, even though management clearly stated that earnings were expected to recover once the transition was complete.

Just another example of irrational shareholder behavior, I thought; so I took advantage and bought in. It took about a month, but surely enough, the price shot back up and I was able to make an easily predictable 3% gain.

You can compare a stock's trailing P/E ratio to its forward P/E ratio to determine if management expects earnings to be lower or higher in the future, compared to the current share price. For example, if you find a company with a 10 trailing P/E ratio and a 20 forward P/E ratio, then you can expect future earnings to be less than past earnings.

It is wise to stay away from these companies. Even though management already informed the shareholders of decreased earnings, they will still go into a selling frenzy when lower earnings actually materialize.

Similarly, if you find a company trading at a 10 trailing P/E ratio and a 5 forward P/E ratio, this is likely a smart investment (if all other factors are in place). Shareholders have not yet pushed the stock price higher relative to the increased earnings projection.

Liquid assets: Generally, as long as the company has more current assets than current liabilities (Current Ratio > 1) then I am fine with it. I do not consider a company with a Current Ratio of 10 to be five times better than one with a Current Ratio of 2.

The *law of diminishing returns* applies here. The higher the Current Ratio, the less incremental benefit received.

Think about it. A company with a Current Ratio of 2 is in a much better financial situation than one trading at 0.5. However, a company trading at 10 is better, but not five times better, than one trading at 2. Will the company trading at 10 really decide to take on a ton of debt all of a sudden, just because it can? Not if there is sane management at the helm.

Generally, higher Current Ratios are better because it means the company will be able to take on debt at lower interest rates if needed. However the ability to take on debt does not give the company a continual tangible benefit such as ROA/ROE.

Let me explain with an example. Consider a company that leads its industry where 10% ROE is average. If the industry leader maintains a 25% ROE, it means the leader utilizes its equity base 2.5 times better than industry average. This provides a continual benefit to the company in the form of high earnings.

Now consider a company that leads its industry where a Current Ratio of 3 is average. If the industry leader maintains a Current Ratio of 12, it does not mean the leader is 4 times more effective than average. It just means the leader will be able to take on more debt if needed. In other words, a higher Current Ratio means one company has more insurance than another does.

Would you rather have a salary of $500,000 per year or a $5 million insurance policy? The $500,000 salary of course – and the reason you would pick it is because even though the insurance policy is great and could help during hard times, it would only help if things turn bad. On the contrary, a $500,000 per year salary provides a continuous benefit to you.

The same concept applies to a company's Current Ratio. A high Current Ratio is good, but do not solely base your investment decision on it. Look for indicators that the company is continually increasing its value, such as maintaining a high ROE/ROA.

Recent price performance: All else being equal, a stock that has made significant recent gains does not have as much room to grow as one that has experienced significant recent losses. This is purely because traders judge a company's current stock price by its historical stock price.

Recall the earlier discussion on trading ranges. A $10 stock that once traded at $30 appears more undervalued than a $20 stock that once traded at $30. This is due to market psychology and is best not to fight it; instead, just understand and adjust to it. In the stock market, everyone is a little fish trying to navigate Niagara Falls. So in this particular case, it is best to flow with the water's current rather than fight against the current.

I like to find strong, undervalued companies that have recently taken a huge price hit compared to their industry. It is like finding out that the hottest girl in class is now single just because she has a pimple; eventually the pimple will be gone and others will realize her true value.

If a stock price has taken an unfounded hit, which was based more on fear than actual company performance, then this is a perfect buy-in opportunity. After investors calm down, they realize the company took an unnecessarily large hit and will buy back in, which pushes the stock up and allows you to sell quickly at a 3% gain.

Every day after market close, I use a spreadsheet to find fundamentally strong companies that took a huge price hit for the day. I evaluate each of these stocks to understand the reason why it took a hit. Generally, it is due to some sort of bad news, however sometimes there is just no obvious explanation.

If there is no bad news out, or if I feel the traders overreacted and sold excessively low, I will buy shares in the after-market as long as the asking price has not bounced back up yet. Usually the stock will correct itself the next day, which gives me a quick 3% gain.

Quick, easy money by taking advantage of people's fear and greed – that is the name of the game.

Let us look at a real example of this strategy at work. After market close on December 18, 2013, I noticed that Jabil Circuit Inc. (JBL) dropped 20% due to news that one of its "major suppliers" had declining demand.

Jabil Circuit produces components for Apple's iPhone, hence when this news was released people panicked at the sheer horror of Apple having declining demand, and sold at extremely low prices. I checked JBL's past income statements, which showed consistent annual earnings in the hundreds of millions. Then I pulled up the past balance sheets, which showed relatively stable net tangible assets of approximately $1.5 billion. Cash flow was good; ROA of 5%; ROA of 17%; approximate P/E of 8 and P/B of 1.5.

Everything looked great, so then I asked the all-important question. Does this news really justify a 20% drop in the company's value?

Did not seem like it. It has been a historically strong company, and Apple is not going anywhere anytime soon. I bought shares in the post market for slightly higher than the day's close. The next day the stock rebounded and hit 3% over my cost basis. See the chart below.

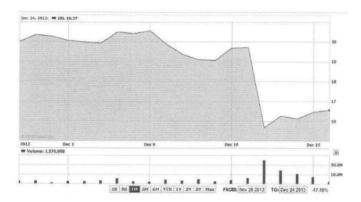

What will this stock do in the future? No one knows, and I certainty do not care because I took my 3% gain and went on to other opportunities.

Could I have held on to this stock and sold a few days later for a slightly better gain? Sure, I know that with 100% certainty now because it is all in hindsight. However I purchased this stock only because I expected a rebound from the irrational sells; this was not an exceptionally undervalued stock compared to its industry.

By holding this stock longer, not only would I have given up better opportunities elsewhere, but would also run the risk that the stock continues dropping out of fear. My next-day 3% gain was not a guaranteed gain. It was a *probable* gain.

Remember there are no perfect buy-in opportunities in the stock market. To become rich you need to keep probability on your side, not take unnecessary risks, and most importantly use the market's random fluctuations to your advantage.

I cannot stress it enough. You can usually expect strong companies with huge price dips to have some sort of rebound; however, you cannot predict how much or how long it will rebound. Take your 3% gain and move on to the next opportunity before you regret not selling when you had the chance.

Similar to my preference of investing during price dips, I rarely invest if the stock price recently shot up, no matter how strong or undervalued the company is. It is very likely that fearful or bored investors will quickly take profits, driving the price back down.

The market is irrational: overvalued stocks can stay overvalued for a while, and undervalued stocks can stay undervalued. Just because the price of an undervalued stock recently spiked up does not mean that investors are finally seeing the light. There is a high likelihood that as quick as it gapped up, it will just as quickly drop back down the next day.

Although we would be fine with holding stock for an undervalued company, our goal is to frequently sell at small gains. We cannot sell if our money is tied up in a strong, but nonetheless, underperforming company.

Price volatility: Even though I saved this one for last, it is just as important as the other essential attributes. Our core strategy is to sell at a 3% gain as quickly as possible. The higher a stock's volatility, the greater its price fluctuations, which means the quicker you will be able to sell the stock.

When you find an undervalued company trading at a high price volatility, it is absolute heaven. High price volatility is a sign of either a thinly traded stock or a stock with erratic, undecided investors. The latter is what you want to find.

A few months ago, I found a stock that was both extremely undervalued and trading erratically. A couple of times since then I have been able to buy this stock after a dip, and then quickly sell at a 3% gain after a spike up. Easy money by taking advantage of people's fear and greed.

No stock is a permanent cash cow though. One day the price will correct itself. This will occur by the price spiking up to the company's true value, or maybe the company begins faltering (thus sending fundamentals down), or volatility cools down.

Until this happens, continue trading the stock. As long as you quickly enter and exit stocks, and have an objective criteria for evaluating investments (do not invest in a stock just because you made money in it before), then you increase your chance of gains and reduce the risk of being stuck holding an unattractive stock.

Diversification strategy: Did you predict 9/11 and the resulting crash of the airline business? No. It was a shock to all of us, and was an especially financially painful surprise to those that had invested their entire portfolio in airline stocks.

Never invest all, or even the majority of your portfolio, into one industry or country. You can never predict these extraordinary events and their resulting impact to the stock market. In addition, be mindful that even though two stocks may not operate in the exact same industry, one industry can still have a direct or indirect effect on the other.

If housing demand crashes, surely you do not want your entire portfolio in residential construction stocks; however you also do not want to be in companies dealing with home appliances, ceramic tile, lumber, carpet, or anything else to do with home construction. Be mindful of how your stocks are indirectly related.

We have already discussed never to invest more than 10% of your portfolio in one stock. This percentage will change depending on the amount of money you have in your portfolio, or the maximum percentage of a single company you are comfortable holding.

For the starting investor I would recommend 5-10% per stock. This percentage would be a lot lower for Warren Buffett, who could purchase an entire company with 10% of his portfolio.

Other key attributes

While the previous attributes make or break investment decisions, the following factors only help push your decision in one direction between two otherwise equal stocks:

Long-term peak or valley: I have already mentioned the importance of evaluating recent price dips and spikes. Another important consideration is determining if the stock is trading at a long-term peak or valley.

Generally, prices fluctuate according to the following factors: On a day-to-day basis, stock movements are influenced by traders' individual situations, thus appear random. On a month-to-month basis, investors compare the current price against historical prices and recent news. On a year-to-year basis, prices follow the company's financial stability, future viability, and the government's monetary and fiscal policies.

When evaluating positions, you should put yourself in the investors' shoes and empathize with their feelings.

Humans are an impatient bunch; we all want quick results. If a stock has been trading flat for a year now, how do you think its investors are feeling? They are anxious to exit the position and get into something profitable, but of course they do not want to take a loss, so they continue holding the stock in hopes that it will increase back to their original cost basis.

You want to avoid investing in these stocks because the investors will not allow quick 3% gains; there is going to be a mad selling rush once the price makes the slightest uptick.

Now imagine if the stock has been in a steady downtrend. How are its long-term investors feeling? They are nervous, holding on to the stock in hopes of a reversal. The more the stock drops, the more fearful they become, which results in irrational selling.

Take a look at the example below, from Yahoo! Finance.

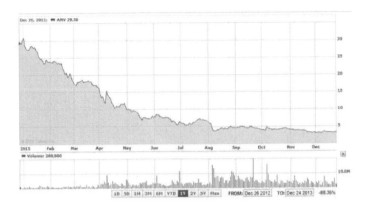

This is a gold mining company. In 2013, gold prices were coming off of all-time highs, which pushed mining stocks down.

This stock started a relatively fast decline in early 2013 based on little volume. This tells you that investors were confident that this company was overpriced.

If investors were not confident in the company's value then you would see the opposite, higher volume with little price change. This situation occurs when pessimistic traders are anxious to sell off their shares at the market price, and optimistic traders are anxious to buy shares at the market price. The end result is high volume with little price change.

You can observe a change of confidence here. By April 2013, the stock price had declined so much that some investors were starting to disagree about the company's worth, as noted by the increasing volume combined with slowing price decline. By September the stock had substantially slowed its decline and was trading relatively flat on very high volume.

This signifies that investors had split opinions on whether this stock was under or overvalued. Split opinions are prime opportunities for our 3% strategy. We do not know how the stock will perform over the long-term, but we know there is a very good chance of small spikes upward as investors try to make up their minds.

Let us consider what would have happened if we entered a position at the beginning of September:

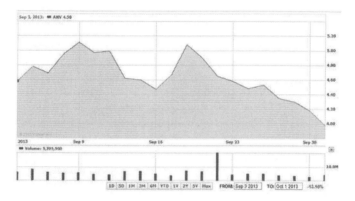

Look at those peaks and valleys within a one-month timeframe! If we had followed our strategy of investing after one of the large dips, we could have made 3% very quickly.

What if we had purchased the stock at the end of September where it dips off? That would have been no problem; refer back to the previous chart to see the large spike up at the beginning of October. As long as we would have sold at a 3% gain in October we would have been quickly out of the position with profit. And is it really so bad if it takes a couple of weeks before hitting a 3% gain? We only invest in fundamentally strong companies; hence, we are not worried about holding a strong company while waiting for a move up.

These are not cherry-picked stocks for the purposes of proving a point. They are all stocks I have profited from using insightful trading. I control the natural urge to hold stocks after hitting 3% gain, and control the urge to sell stocks upon a small dip. This is what allows me to make continual, successful trades in the market.

Percentage of shares shorted: The more a stock is shorted the more its price is artificially lowered compared to an equal, non-shorted stock. Eventually these shares will be bought back, which raises the price back to a normal level.

Short-squeeze is a term used in the situation where a price increase causes short-sellers to cover their positions, either out of fear of losing substantial money or because they do not have enough funds to cover the maintenance call.

The more heavily a stock is shorted, the greater the potential impact of a short-squeeze. This does not mean that a short-squeeze has a higher probability of occurrence, but that, if a short-squeeze occurs, the stock price will have a larger rise up.

It is like comparing a 5-year-old boy pulling a slingshot back versus Hulk Hogan pulling it back. Which person is going to send the rock the furthest distance?

Stocks with over 20% shares short are heavily shorted. It is important to understand why the stock is heavily shorted before investing. Sometimes the short sellers are betting on a particularly negative situation to pan out, possibly bad news or bad earnings. If it is probable that trouble is looming for the company, do not invest. Investing in this situation would be relying on luck, and there are better opportunities out there where luck is not required.

Short sellers have a tendency to behave as a group of starved leeches in a bayou. They move as a group; latching onto a particular stock and not letting go until burned off by a massive short squeeze. Besides directly depressing stock prices through the act of short selling, they indirectly depress prices by scaring off would-be investors.

Much like the mafia, short sellers rely on fear to make money. Stocks tend to fall faster and harder due to fear. Short sellers realize this and hope they can enter a short position in a stock that has potential to take a huge dip from fear.

They attempt to scare investors by posting negative rumors (or even lies) about the company throughout Internet message boards. These negative postings can significantly harm a company and its shareholders.

I have seen short sellers write articles on popular investment websites accusing companies of large-scale fraud, while providing little or no evidence to back up these claims.

The article spreads throughout the media and is posted to investment websites. Investors see these articles and become extremely fearful. This sends the stock price in a downward spiral, which then triggers a slew of lawyers that begin soliciting for lead plaintiffs in a lawsuit against the company. These solicitations also get picked up by media outlets, causing more fear and sending the price down further.

Eventually trading is halted on the stock for a couple of months while investigations are conducted. If the company is innocent, then the halt is lifted and the price eventually trends to a fair value; but this takes a while.

The more short sellers in a stock, the more negative sentiment will be posted about the company. The more negative sentiment, the harder it will be for the stock to frequently hit 3% gains.

Remember that many people invest in a herd mentality; they feel more comfortable fitting in with society than going against society. A casual investor researching a particular stock is less likely to invest if he finds a slew of negative sentiment about the company. Whether true or not, these negative sentiments scare-off would-be investors, or lower investor's excitement about the stock, which reduces the likelihood of upwards price spikes.

A highly shorted stock has the potential for a huge upswing from a short-squeeze, but also has the potential to tie-up your money for months. So how does this affect our trading strategy?

Understand that for a short-squeeze to occur, short sellers have to become fearful. For this to happen, good news needs to come out, sending the price upwards, which causes shorts to begin covering their positions. If good news is driving the price up anyway, then this good news alone will probably drive the price up at least 3% for you to sell. Any other gain over 3% caused by a short squeeze is inconsequential to you because you have already sold your position.

Investors who enter long positions just because the stock is heavily shorted are betting that a short-squeeze will offer a huge gain upwards. This is definitely a possibility, however the halted trading scenario I previously described is also a possibility.

So we have two potential outcomes from a heavily shorted stock: long-term depressed prices or the chance of an upwards surge. Considering these outcomes, a heavily shorted stock is slightly less valuable than a lightly shorted stock. However this factor alone would not keep me from entering a long position if I feel the stock is underpriced and is likely to spike up soon.

In a later section I will discuss if, and when, short-selling is an optimal strategy. For now we are focused on buys.

Percentage of shares owned by institutions/insiders: Institutions and insiders are two parties that generally trade for the long-term. Institutions are bound by bureaucratic rules that discourage frequent buying/selling. Insiders are naturally pressured towards buying and holding stocks; frequent day trading opens them up to SEC investigations and shareholder scrutiny, both of which they want to avoid.

It is less probable that panic selling, and just selling in general, will occur if institutions and insiders own a large percentage of the company. This promotes strong support in the share price, and if the company continues doing well it is probable that insiders and institutions will continue buying.

A large and growing insider ownership base reassures investors on the company's stability and financial statement accuracy. Insiders are not going to invest their own money into a company they know is fraudulent or gloomy.

Although percentage of shares owned by institutions/insiders does not make or break a company, if choosing between two equal stocks I would recommend entering one with the higher percentage. The biggest hindrance to our 3% strategy is a stock that takes a huge or long-term price dip. Investing in a stock primarily owned by long-term traders reduces the risk that these price dips will occur.

Dividend yield: Few companies pay dividends, but investors enjoy them because they perceive it as free money. You can make arguments for or against paying dividends. Personally I think they are a poor use of cash for two reasons.

First, they are subject to double taxation (company pays taxes on income, the shareholders again pay taxes on the dividend derived from the income).

Second, a stock price usually drops on the ex-dividend date to reflect the dividend having been paid. Since the company does not have the cash on-hand anymore and it is too late for new investors to receive the dividend, it makes the stock less attractive to new investors.

Many people do not think this deep into things (surprise). They perceive a dividend as easy money in their pocket.

I would prefer that a company use its excess cash for growth, or at the very least for repurchasing shares if the stock is undervalued. If the company has no attractive projects to pursue and shares are trading at a high price, then I am fine with a dividend. But I would not be ecstatic.

So how does a dividend affect our 3% strategy? A consistent dividend provides investors with an incentive to purchase shares. If you invest in a dividend paying company and the share price suddenly tumbles, there is a higher likelihood that the share price will recover faster than a non-dividend company. All else equal of course.

Remember, dividend yield is important, not payout ratio. The payout ratio is the percentage of earnings paid out as dividends. If a company with $1 million in earnings pays out $100k of that, its payout ratio will be 10%. If the company has 100k shares outstanding, trading at $50 each, then the $100k dividend is divided among the 100k shares, with each share receiving $1. The dividend yield is $1/$50, or 2%.

Another company with $10 million in earnings that pays out $500k in dividends will have a payout ratio of 5%. If the company also has 100k shares outstanding trading at $50 each, then the $500k dividend is paid out against 100k shares, so each share receives $5. The dividend yield is $5/$50, or 10%.

In this case, the shareholders of the company with the lower payout ratio actually receive more cash than the company with the higher payout ratio. So remember to evaluate stocks based on dividend yield, which is the amount of cash each shareholder had to spend in order to receive a certain amount back in dividends.

Cash flow: The cash flow statement is useful to understand if, and how, the company is handling incoming and outgoing funds that are not represented on the income statement.

A company can have positive net income with negative cash flow, meaning that the company booked profits for the period; however, these profits did not actually make it into the company's bank as cash. This occurs when a company uses its money for activities such as investments, capital asset expenditures, debt repayment, or repurchasing shares.

Some industries are more capital-intensive than others. Airlines, construction companies, and mining companies all require a great deal of capital in order to make a profit. Most of an airline's capital is invested in airplanes. Imagine what would happen if that airline company stopped purchasing and repairing its airplanes. They would have to serve less and less customers over time, eventually going bankrupt.

Now imagine the scenario where the airline company adequately purchases and maintains its aircraft; however less people choose to fly. The airline cannot sell its aircraft fleet or reduce maintenance just because the customer base is declining. Selling aircraft would mean less available flights, which would lead to even more business decline.

And certainly it cannot reduce maintenance on an aircraft just because less people fly in it.

Therefore airline companies, like other capital-intensive companies, must maintain high asset utilization rates in order to sustain profitability. If the assets must be used anyway, then it is better to use them more rather than less.

If you observe that a mining company has not made any capital purchases within the last three years, you would question if it has been maintaining its equipment. If it has not, then the company could later be hit with a large financial impact when it finally does replace its equipment; its cash will be used to replace existing equipment rather than expand the business.

Another helpful section on the cash flow statement is "Cash flow from financing activities." Here you want to look for instances of stock dilution (positive "Sale Purchase of Stock" line item) and new debt incurred (positive "Net Borrowings" line item).

Before investing in a company, you want to ensure it is not frequently diluting its shareholders or incurring new debt. Either one of these signifies that the company is not generating enough earnings to pull its own weight; management has to draw from one of two financial wells.

The cash flow statement also allows you to understand management's financial philosophy. Do they prefer diluting shareholders rather than taking on new debt? If so, it is possible the company has so much debt already that it cannot afford to take on more. This is a situation where insider ownership is important. Management will take shareholder-friendly actions if they are the main shareholders.

Either way, if a company frequently finances itself by means other than earning income on its operations, it would benefit you to stay away from it. There are plenty of other companies that can pay their bills using income they worked for, rather than borrowed.

Investor sentiment: Before purchasing stock I like to understand how other people are perceiving the company; both the criticism and the praise. A quick way to do this is checking message boards.

Understand that people post a lot of garbage on message boards. Ninety percent of posts are people trying to convince others how wonderful or horrible the stock is.

Those bashing the stock are short sellers trying to instill fear within the investment community. As previously discussed, the more shares shorted, the more fear-mongering posts you will find.

Another frequent behavior is speculators trying to convince others to keep buying at higher and higher prices; not because they believe it is in the best interest of others, but because the speculators are controlled by their own greed. They hope to convince others to buy the stock at higher prices in a desperate attempt to sell their own stock at a higher price. This is especially prevalent after the stock price has been on a steady uptrend.

Ignore the fear-mongers and speculators. They try to persuade you to trade in a manner that will make them rich, not make you rich. These people are easy to spot; their posts are of no substance and contain at least one exclamation mark.

Speculators will arbitrarily name an unrealistically high price that they "predict" the stock to reach while the fear-mongers will claim the company is engaged in fraud and mock long investors. Speculators and fear-mongers make these statements without any support (if either individual is going to make such claims, at least post some sort of logical proof).

The other 10% of posts are investors trying to understand if the stock is a wise investment decision. These are the only posts you should pay attention to because they logically discuss the company's current affairs.

Different stocks will have different classes of investors. Before entering a position, consider how you can use their weaknesses to your advantage.

Casual investors with unrefined business acumen will close their eyes, think of the big brand today, and buy a few shares.

Specifically, the casual younger generation gravitates towards the social media scene such as Facebook, Twitter, and LinkedIn. They invest in these companies because they have witnessed their success and think (incorrectly) that recently successful companies are the best investments.

In actuality, social media companies are some of the worst to invest in because they are usually overpriced with uncertain continuity. Remember MySpace? For about three years, it was the leading social media website and one of the most visited websites in the world. It did not stay on top for long, as Facebook later overtook it in 2008 as the leading social media website. At that time, Facebook was the cool thing for teenagers to participate in.

Now six years later, the teenager's parents and grandparents are all on Facebook which makes it not so cool anymore. Expect to see a demographics shift for Facebook within the next few years, as teenagers move into other social media outlets that are marketed directly for teenagers. Ironically, the older generation will become Facebook's strongest customer base.

The casual older generation prefers investing in stable companies they grew up with, such as General Electric, Proctor & Gamble, and Johnson & Johnson. These stocks are less speculative, however usually remain overvalued based on their strong brand name, thus are not the most ideal investments.

Experienced investors have a wider variety of strategies. Notice I did not say a smarter variety – just a wider variety. They have played the markets long enough to develop their own strategies over time, and long-term experience makes them believe that they have the best strategies out there. Even though they have more experience, I venture to say that the 80/20 rule still applies here. Eighty percent of these investors make only 20% of the profits. A small number of insightful investors make the bulk of profits.

Older, experienced investors that were around long enough to live through the rampant inflation of the 1970s know the value of gold. These investors will flock towards gold at the slightest hint of increased money printing. This is generally a good strategy because in effect, our society has created a rule that when inflation rises, buy gold.

On other planets, gold and a funny smelling green paper will never be substitute goods. However things are different in our world. People are naturally drawn to the beauty of gold; however they are more drawn to green paper because it can buy anything, including gold.

But green paper is, in fact, just green paper. Sometimes this makes the holders of green paper nervous; they begin wondering how they will survive if suddenly no one wants their paper anymore. This nervousness causes them to trade green paper for gold, which will always be in demand.

This psychology will cause gold to continue dipping and spiking as along as the world economy exists. No matter how many times you hear people toting the absurd statement that gold is no more, it is merely ignorance speaking.

Humans have a natural attraction to gold that has existed for thousands of years; this will never change. Do you know where most gold comes from? It is formed from the intense heat and pressure of neutron star collisions. Seen any neutron star collisions lately? That should tell you that there is a limited supply of gold.

The world population is increasing. What happens when an increasing population all desire the same, non-renewable resource that is delivered via rare, uncontrollable stellar events?

It sounds like gold prices are only going to increase.

Speaking of increasing prices, the value of the dollar has been consistently decreasing year after year, right?

So you have a green piece of paper that has been around a few years and continually loses value, then you have a limited mineral that has been desired worldwide for thousands of years. When the green paper loses value, it takes more green paper to buy the same piece of gold. In turn, this increases the gold prices.

See where I am going with this? Gold is here to stay, and will increase in value over the long-term. Do not let the ignorant loudmouths tell you otherwise just because gold is in a short-term price dip. They are the same people that will short sell an undervalued, financially strong company just because it "appears" to be downtrending.

We got a little sidetracked on the gold discussion, however it is a widely spoken topic and deserved its own mention. The main point I want you to take away is that the same concept can apply to other precious metals and stocks.

Do not be fooled by short-term price dips. Use logical thinking. If the precious metal is limited and desired enough, its price will go up in the long-term. Likewise, if a company's goods or services are limited and desired enough, its price will go up in the long-term.

Overall, use investor sentiment to help you understand a company from those people who closely follow the company. And maintain your composure; do not let the fear-mongers and speculators sway you their way.

Earnings season: Stock prices tend to become more volatile immediately before and after earning announcements.

Prior to the announcement, there is great uncertainty. People with unrealized gains are pressured to take them while they still can; those holding an unprofitable stock are hoping that a great quarter pushes the price up and allows them to sell for a gain.

Due to this uncertainty, it is best to stay away from purchases prior to earning announcements. You may wonder, isn't volatility something good that we always seek?

Yes, normal day-to-day volatility is how we make our money, however earnings volatility is a different beast. No one knows what kind of numbers the company will release. They could be good numbers which make the stock all the more undervalued, or they can be horrendous numbers that immediately change the company's fundamentals.

Would you be happy if you invested in a company that you thought was undervalued, only to have an earnings release that turns your undervalued company into just an average company?

On the other hand, while it is risky to purchase stocks immediately before an earnings release, after earnings release is hunting season. Companies that did not meet expectations are sold off so quickly that you think they had just announced bankruptcy.

Purchasing after an irrational price dip due to missed earnings is the second best opportunity to buy in cheap (the first being a significant, random dip).

Ask yourself, did the negative earnings report justify the amount of price drop that occurred? Usually the answer will be no. If the company reported 10% lower earnings than expected and only foresees this as a one-time drop, while the stock value sunk 25%, then you know that investors overreacted. Buy in cheap now. Once the irrational people had time to calm down and realize it is not the end of the world, they will buy back in at higher prices. Easy profit for you.

Executive pay: If you owned stock of a company that could barely pay its bills, would you be a little agitated that the CEO was banking $5 million per year?

When executives make outrageously high salaries compared to the company size and its performance, this is a red flag. It infers two things: 1) Management has little incentive to improve company performance because they are already well paid; and 2) The Board is incompetent enough to allow the CEO such a high salary for poor performance.

On the contrary, if executive pay is strongly linked to company performance via stock options, then I am more comfortable that management will be properly motivated to improve company performance.

Management's tone: Using a 3% strategy, you do not stay in a company long enough to become familiar with the company's executives. This makes it difficult to form educated opinions on their leadership strategy.

Some investors believe that it is essential to study company executives before investing. I say that is bunch of phooey. Spending time learning executive's backgrounds, the schools they attended, previous workplaces, reading entire transcripts – these are all wasted activities that take you away from doing something more worthwhile, like spending time with your family.

No matter how much you study an executive, you will never know him personally or work with him on a daily basis. And surely you will never get into his head to read his emotions and understand his true intentions. Even personally knowing someone is not enough to base an investment decision on. Think of all the businesspeople, politicians, and regular people that end up shocking their closest friends and family with scandals.

Overanalyzing anything in the market, including company management, will only increase <u>confidence</u> in your abilities; it will not increase the abilities themselves. The more confidence you have, the more chance that greed will drive your decisions.

That does not mean you should totally ignore management. Take a few seconds to read how management explains earning results. Do they explain things clear and in layman terms to provide transparency to the investors? Or do they simply state the facts without providing any sort of explanation to the shareholders? Take a look at Warren Buffett's annual letters to Berkshire Hathaway shareholders. Buffett provides complete transparency to shareholders, even telling them when he believes Berkshire stock is overpriced. His letters are the essence of honest management.

If company management does not take the time to clearly explain the company's strengths, weaknesses, opportunities, and threats – is it because management does not know these factors, does not care enough about the shareholders to explain them, or are they hiding other intentions?

Whichever way you slice it, this type of management is poisonous to a company. I strongly hesitate investing in a company where management does not provide adequate disclosure to its owners.

So far we have focused on how to select stocks for purchasing. What about short selling? Do insightful investors ever bet against a company? All the answers are coming up.

Part IV – Bonds, short selling, options, and other fetishes: Using contrarian behavior as insurance against irrational markets

The complexity of an investor's research has a strong, positive correlation to his market ignorance.

We have discussed long stock positions but have not yet touched upon the multitude of other "strategies" out there. Although frequent 3% gains are the core to becoming a billionaire, it is wise to become familiar with other opportunities. Understanding the big picture, whether or not you choose to participate in it, will allow you to better understand society's behavior.

Bonds

Bonds are the annoying tag-along brother to stocks. When schmoozers are awkwardly united together at a business gathering that is bound to destroy more brain cells than actually acquiring knowledge, the topic of investments is bound to arise. And when it does, nearly every introduction begins with, "So...uh...Tim... do you invest in stocks and bonds?"

While there can be thrilling conversations on stock picks, not one single soul is interested in another's 30-year, 5% Pennsylvania Power Systems General Obligation Municipal bond callable at 104.

Next time someone asks about your stock and bond investments, have a little fun by naming random, made-up bonds. If he does not walk away from boredom after a few seconds, press him harder and say that you only invest in AAA-rated bonds with coupon rates in the 18-20% range. If you get an "ah-hah", or "interesting" remark, you have just confirmed his schmoozer status with absolutely no investment knowledge.

So why are unsexy bonds always mentioned in the same sentence as stocks?

Bonds are widely considered to be the safe investment alternative to stocks. For the individual investor, it feels almost sacrilege to invest your entire portfolio in stocks with no bonds strewn in there. For mutual funds and other managed investment advisors, *it is* sacrilege to invest a client's entire portfolio in stocks.

People feel uncomfortable having their entire net worth in the stock market. After all, what would they do if the unspeakable thing happens, such as their prized company declares bankruptcy?

First, investing your money into bonds to avoid bankruptcies or market crashes is the same thing as never leaving your house for fear of a deadly car crash. You are avoiding death by choosing a boring life. With bonds, you forego becoming rich just to ensure that you can receive a few pennies back on the dollar during a bankruptcy.

Remember, bonds are not 100% risk-free. Just like stocks, bonds are contingent on the issuer's health. If the issuer declares bankruptcy, both stockholders and bondholders lose. The only difference is that bondholders are entitled to their cash (whatever is left of it) before stockholders.

Who are these people investing in such bankruptcy-prone companies anyway? Sure, every company has a chance to go bankrupt, however bankruptcy is not something that happens overnight. You have to hold onto a strong stock for a long, long time before it turns into a bankrupt mess.

Who holds a failing company this long? People that cannot come to grip with reality. Similar to our earlier investor who was just a few short years away from retirement; these people continue pouring money into a sinking hole out of fear.

The lower risk that bonds offer is inconsequential because we only invest in financially strong companies. We do not stay around in one company long enough to see it go from very profitable, to somewhat profitable, to neutral, to unprofitable, to distress, to illiquidity. We get out after earning a 3% gain. Therefore, it does not matter if a once profitable company sinks down to illiquidity five years later. We stopped investing in this company long ago after it stopped being undervalued.

One advantage of bonds is that they provide a consistent return on your investment year after year.

Hah, sorry, I had to throw in that joke to keep you on your toes.

If you are willing to forego becoming rich in the market just so that you can feel comfortable earning a consistent 5% per year, then you are reading the wrong book. Someone may brag that they are in an investment-grade bond paying a consistent 5% per year. How cute. I earn more than that each month, compounded, to boot.

Moreover, this person is actually not earning a consistent 5% per year. When inflation rises to 5%, he earns nothing.

Stocks, on the other hand, perform much better during inflationary periods than bonds. When inflation rises, people spend more money, companies report better earnings, valuation ratios drop, stocks become undervalued, and people invest more.

Another threat to bonds comes from our own Federal Reserve System. Consider what happens when the Federal Reserve thinks that inflation is getting out of control. They decide to raise interest rates to 6% in an attempt to reduce the money supply. Now that 5% bond does not look so great anymore, does it?

And what happens if interest rates fall to 1%? Now that 5% bond is a pain in the rear for the issuer, so the issuer calls back the 5% bond and refinances at 1%. The (former) bondholder is left with only a portion of the cash he expected to make over the bond's life. He has to either reinvest this money into a new bond, unfortunately now selling at 1%, or learn how to handle himself in the stock market.

Bottom line is that while bonds may be optimal for passive investors, they are useless for insightful investors. We use market psychology and business acumen to get rich; we do not waste our money on bonds. The safety net of bonds is overrated. Picking the right stocks can get you close or even exceeding the safety of bonds when considering inflation and interest rate risk.

My portfolio is 100% allocated to a diversified range of companies and industries, all within different countries. If one company goes bankrupt out of no-where, so what? I have a dozen other undervalued companies that I am making great money from. If the market crashes, so what? Not only am I invested in very safe stocks that will eventually recover, but I also have a couple of short positions or put options on overvalued companies.

By investing in the most undervalued companies, and entering bearish positions on the most overvalued companies, my portfolio is optimized to outperform both bull and bear markets. Hopefully yours will be too.

Short selling

Refer back to the historical NASDAQ chart from Part II, this time focusing on the *length* of the bull and bear markets:

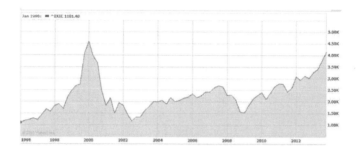

Looking at this chart, it is apparent the NASDAQ moves up more often than moving down. Specifically, since the NASDAQ opened in February 1971 until December 2013, it has risen 59% of the months and fell 41% of the months.

In the up-months the NASDAQ averaged a 4.85% price gain over the previous month; in the down-months it averaged a 4.63% price loss over the previous month.

These statistics show that, overall, the market trends upwards both in duration and magnitude. Inflation further ensures that the market will rise over the long-term.

Of course there will be deviations (market corrections) from this upward trend; these are usually the result of over-speculation or an impending credit crisis. Short selling can help reduce financial losses during these corrections and can even result in nice gains. However, keep in mind that when short selling you are betting against the trend. Betting against the trend is betting against probability, therefore it is unwise to hold large short positions.

Short selling has other disadvantages. It must be performed in margin accounts which results in interest charges. This means you have to experience larger gains from short selling just to equal the gains of a normal long position. In addition, you have the potential for unlimited loss in a short sale, compared with limited losses in a long position.

Considering these risks, it is easy to understand why stocks should rarely be shorted. Significantly undervalued companies will exist in all kinds of markets, so why would you enter a short position that has a lower expected value than a long position?

Having said that, I do think it is sensible to allocate a percentage of your portfolio in bearish positions, especially when the market is significantly overvalued.

Take for example the late 1990s dot-com bubble. If you were able to isolate yourself from the rampant speculation and recognized the market could not sustain such immensely inflated prices, you could have entered a few bearish positions as a hedge against a collapse. You would have earned a great deal of money on these bearish positions when the market crashed.

Notice I am using the words "bearish positions" and not "short selling." I rarely recommend short selling because it risks unlimited loss for a limited gain. However if you are confident that the market (or a particular stock) is significantly overvalued, then it may be wise to purchase a put option to hedge against a market downturn. Options will be discussed shortly.

Inverse ETFs

You could also choose to invest in Inverse Exchange Traded Funds (ETFs), which short the market while eliminating the risk of losing more than your original investment. The downside is that these ETFs are not ideal for long-term holding. As we covered earlier the market has a tendency to increase; therefore the longer you hold these ETFs, the greater the chance of losing money. It is the same concept as gambling in a casino. You may win in the short-term, but the longer you play the more you deviate towards odds that are highly stacked against you.

Also consider that the more stocks that comprise an inverse ETF, the greater the chance that the ETF will follow the overall market, which is up. Since the main selling point of ETFs is that it is a single security comprised of multiple short sales or derivatives, you can easily see that they are not ideal for your portfolio.

Bearish positions should not comprise the majority of your portfolio; they should only be used as a hedge against market downturns. You have no idea when the market will drop; it could be days, months, or years from now. You will lose a lot of money holding inverse ETFs waiting for the market to crash.

So how should one hold a bearish position? Enter stock options.

Stock options

A put option gives you the opportunity to sell a stock at a predefined price. If you believe a stock is significantly overvalued at $100/share, you may pay a $2 premium to purchase a put option that allows you to sell the stock at $95/share.

Options are usually sold in lots of 100, so you will pay $200 ($2 * 100) for the option to sell this stock at $95/share. In order to break even the stock price would have to drop to $93/share (you receive $9500 from the stock, minus $200 for the option), excluding commissions.

Buying puts in lieu of outright short selling reduces much of the risk associated with short selling. Of course, when purchasing options the stock has to drop enough to yield a profit plus the cost of the option. However I would much rather be out the cost of the option versus some freak short selling situation where the stock price increases ten-fold and I am left selling my house to pay a margin call.

You should purchase puts that have an expiration date very far in the future. These will cost more, however you do not know when the stock price will come crashing down; it could be tomorrow or months from now. Since the market has a tendency to go up more than it goes down, it is probable that a market crash will happen later rather than sooner.

Option trading is not available for every stock on the market. In rare situations, you may "need to" short a stock if you want to take a bearish position. You should only do this in situations where a stock is obviously in a bubble and you are 99.98% sure it will come crashing down.

A personal example, I entered a short position on a stock that had no earnings, a market value of $2 billion, a self-calculated P/E ratio of -100,000; a P/B of 600; and no prospects for increased growth.

This was a bubble waiting to burst, and I needed a bearish position anyway to hedge against the currently overpriced market. Nevertheless, I was still hesitant about shorting it because, as Warren Buffett says, the market can be irrational longer than you can be solvent.

After shorting this stock (putting no more than 10% of my portfolio value, mind you), the stock price began increasing even more. Over two weeks it had increased 25% over my cost basis. Would anyone have thought that a stock that was so overpriced to begin with, could increase 25% on top of that? Well, it can happen. Luckily, I followed my own strategy of not allocating over 10% of my portfolio in this short sell.

It has fell since then and is sitting at 15% over my cost basis. I am still confident it will come crashing down; I just do not know when. I am telling you this as a caution against going on a mad shorting spree. If you have to short stock, it is better to short a few stocks a modest amount of money rather than one stock for a significant amount.

You want to keep about 10% of your portfolio in bearish positions during normal market conditions and up to 20% during an extremely overvalued market; however you should use put options as much as possible.

We already discussed buying put options. What about selling put and call options, and buying call options?

Selling put options is an unnecessary risk. This means you are selling the option for someone else to sell a stock to you at a specific price. If the price skyrockets, then you do not have to worry about the buyer executing her put option because she will not sell to you at a lower price than the stock is currently worth.

The other scenario is that the price crashes to nothing. Now she is more than willing to unload her worthless stock onto you for a high price. And since you sold the option you have no choice but to buy the worthless stock from her.

The most you can lose from selling put options is the entire stock value minus the premium received. For example, if you sell one put option that allows the buyer to sell ABC stock to you at $50/share, in effect you are selling her the right to sell you $5,000 worth of ABC stock. You may charge her a $2/share premium for this option, meaning she pays you $200 for the option. As long as the stock price stays above $48, she will not execute her option. However if the stock price falls to nothing, she will execute her option and you will be forced to buy the stock at $50/share, or $5,000. Ultimately, you realize a $4,800 loss.

Now consider buying a call option. This means you are buying the option to purchase stock at a specific price. Why would you want to buy the option to purchase stock when you can just buy it now at the market price?

Think of it as a layaway payment that you may or may not get back.

For example, consider a trader that only has $500 available in his brokerage account. This is not enough money to purchase a significant portion of the stock he wants, but he thinks the stock will soon skyrocket up and does not want to miss out. Therefore, he will pay someone $200 for the option to later purchase 100 shares of stock at a specific price. If he later decides to execute this option, he needs to have enough available cash in his account.

The kind of people that use this strategy are the same kind that use those cash advance checks they receive in the mail. Do not be one of those people.

Besides acting as layaway, there are other reasons why a trader would purchase a call option. He may be convinced that a stock will make a large move up or down, pending an earnings release. He does not want to take the risk of buying the stock then watching it tank to nothing, nor does he want to take the risk of shorting the stock and watching it shoot to the moon. In this situation he decides to buy both a call and a put option. If he is correct and it makes a significant move one way, then he profits.

By now you should know that this is a horrible strategy. You are paying the price of two options all the while betting the stock will move enough to recover the option costs. No one can predict how much a stock price will move.

Consider the situation where a negative earnings report comes out, sending the stock price downward. Right before reaching the point where you are able to execute your put option for a profit, our New York millionaire sits down at his computer, thinks to himself "What a great buy!" and purchases all shares trading at that price which sends the stock price rebounding back up. Now you are stuck holding two worthless options.

The third and most useful situation to buy a call option is to hedge a short sale position. Assume you are confident that a stock price will tank, however you do not want to buy a put option. You short the stock then buy a call option in order to limit your potential loss. If the stock shoots up past the call option breakeven point, you execute the call option and cover your short position for a limited loss.

However it is very possible that you enter into a short position, buy a call option expiring in three months, and then the stock trades sideways for three months. Now you have a worthless option and an unhedged short position. You will have to purchase another call option to continue hedging your risk. This can go on indefinitely if the stock continues trading sideways.

You may be wondering, why not just buy a put option instead? I agree with you. Those who hedge a short position with a call, rather than purchase a put, are usually the more speculative traders.

Put options are more expensive than call options because a put seller takes on more risk than a covered call seller does. So some people would rather pay little for a call option, short the stock, and bet that the stock price will fall hard and fast enough to make this strategy worthwhile.

Covered call seller? This is a trader who already owns the stock that he is selling a call option for. If he sells a call without owning the stock, that is referred to selling a naked call, and is an unnecessarily risky tactic. Would you ever promise to sell something you do not even own, at a specific price? You will not get much sleep if you sold a naked call on a $5 stock that suddenly gapped upward to $100/share, when the call buyer then decided that it was now a good time to purchase that stock you promised him at $5/share.

By now if you think I am against options, you are mostly correct. However selling covered calls is not all that bad. You can use them to earn a little extra while waiting for your stocks to hit a 3% gain. Here is an example of covered call selling.

A trader is holding a $10 stock and needs it to hit $13 in order to realize a 3% gain. Instead of letting that stock sit around in his portfolio, he decides to sell someone the option to purchase the stock at $12, for a $1 premium. So the call buyer needs the stock to hit at least $13 before executing his call. If the option expires without the stock hitting $13, then the call seller pockets $1/share.

If the stock passes $13 before the option expires then he has to sell the stock for $13. But that was the plan anyway, right? This is why covered call selling fits in with our 3% strategy. We either make extra money when the call option expires worthless, or we sell the stock for the same price we would have sold it for anyway.

Sounds too good to be true? Well, there is a catch.

First off, it is difficult to sell call options at a price that yields a quick 3% gain. The demand for call options is just not that high.

Secondly, consider the situation where you sell a $1 covered call at a $12 strike price, expiring in three months. After a week the stock reaches $13. Great – take it off my hands, please! Not so fast. The call buyer decides he does not want to exercise the option just yet. The stock price dwindles back down to $10 and never goes back up to $13. Well you made $100 on the expired call three months later, but you missed your chance to make a 3% gain after a week.

Then consider the situation where you need to get out of the stock at a 2.95% gain versus a 3% gain. Possibly the stock spiked up 2.95% one morning and you would like to take this gain and reinvest in an undervalued stock that just took a 10% dip. You cannot sell these shares though; they are tied up in a covered call until the expiration date.

Therefore when selling covered calls, remember to not lose sight of the ultimate objective of selling at 3% gains. Although you may earn a nice premium selling covered calls expiring in a year, you do not want to be on the hook for a year. You will be foregoing a large amount of compounding interest just to collect one premium.

For this reason I only sell covered calls expiring in a week or two. Sure, it is rare to find someone who is willing to pay a 3% premium to buy an option expiring in a week, however the ability to sell at quick 3% gains is much more important than collecting a premium.

Overall, I recommend just sticking with buying the occasional put. Do not get caught up in the speculation of selling puts or naked calls. People experience actual drug-like highs (dopamine bursts) by continually selling these sort of options because they result in immediate cash collection. Unfortunately, you run the same risk as when you frequently purchase on credit. You will be on the hook for huge payouts that can break your finances.

Identifying bearish positions

Bullish trading is much easier than bearish trading. In bullish trading you are investing with the market's natural momentum. Think of it as riding a raft where the current simply carries you to your destination. Of course you can get there faster with a good paddle, however the current will still take you there regardless of your paddle size.

Although helpful, this characteristic makes a bull market dangerous. Many traders become overconfident in their strategies during a bull market because they experience most of their wins during this time. Again, this is why you should always use a sensible, not speculative, trading strategy.

Conversely, bearish trading is similar to riding a raft against the current. In this case, the current is your worst enemy, and without a good paddle you will be swept down into the waterfall's abyss.

To add to your disadvantage, there are not many good paddles available. And you will find that many paddles look fine on first glance, however their weakness will later manifest when the paddle breaks from the current's intense pressure.

If you cannot find a strong paddle (significantly overvalued stock) then do not try to travel against the current. If you do find that rare strong paddle, do not discard it until you find a stronger replacement.

When entering a bearish position your number one priority is survival, not frequent gains. Bullish positions are ideal for frequent trading because you have two advantages to your disposal: an undervalued company and the market's upward flow. With bearish positions you are missing half of this advantage, so you should only devote a small portion of your portfolio to bearish positions as a hedge against a market crash.

Consider your bearish positions as insurance; their sole purpose is to mitigate an unexpected disaster to your portfolio. They are not to meant to make money, in fact they can sometimes be a cost.

To identify bearish opportunities, recall back to the strategies used to identify bullish opportunities. Many of these concepts can be reversed to select a bearish opportunity. Normally you will only devote 10% of your portfolio to bearish positions; therefore you should select only the most overvalued stocks in the market.

The market is filled with gamblers who have no reservation about buying and holding overvalued stocks for a long period of time. Gamblers will firmly hold a position unless fear causes them to dump the stock, and even in this case it is still very difficult to convince a gambler to stop gambling. Gamblers, when faced with surmounting losses, will respond by just gambling more.

Keep this concept in mind when browsing potential bearish opportunities. Gamblers do not fear stocks on a consistent uptrend, no matter how overvalued they are. They also do not fear speculative companies or those with weak financial positions. As long as the stock price is performing well, gamblers love it.

On the other hand, gamblers fear stocks with exponentially decreasing prices. They also fear companies with inconsistent earnings (notice I said inconsistent earnings, not negative earnings).

A company with negative earnings can actually fare better than a company with inconsistent earnings. Uncertainty is the biggest fear driver in the market. If traders expect a company to have negative $1 million earnings and this later proves accurate, then there will be no surprise and the price will remain stable. However if traders expect positive $10 million earnings and the company only makes $5 million, the stock price will tank.

After bad news is released on a company, its stock price will drop so much that it now trades for less than its weaker counterparts, even considering the effect of the news. Fundamentally this does not make sense, however psychologically it does. Remember that market fluctuations are one big circle. Everyone trades based on what they think others will do. This is why short-term market prices are not very rational.

Irrationality allows you to find undervalued companies that spike up 3% in a short-term; however this same irrationality can take continual bites out of your bearish positions. This is why you should purchase puts rather than short selling; an irrational bull market can wipeout a portfolio filled with shorted stocks.

There are two types of companies that you can enter a bearish position in: 1) An immensely overvalued company; or 2) An insolvent company.

No matter whether you choose option #1 or #2, you need to be reasonably confident that the stock price will fall out of fear. Unlike the strategies used to enter a bullish position, where some attributes are optional and can be used to help decide between two positions, all attributes are required to be perfect when entering a bearish position.

Immensely overvalued companies have ridiculous P/B, P/Cash, and P/E ratios. When I say ridiculous, I am speaking in terms relevant to their industry, but generally companies with a P/B and P/Cash over 50, and a P/E over 200 (or a 0 P/E with huge losses) can be considered ridiculously overvalued.

Take care when evaluating companies based on these ratios. It is possible that the ratios are so high because of an unusual, one-off year. Consequently, you want to check the company's forward P/E ratio or projected EPS change, which tells you how well the company thinks it will do in the future. Learn to trust these projections. While it is possible that the company is just overestimating their future earnings, you do not want to bet against their Financial Reporting Department. They know their company a lot better than you do.

After finding a grossly overvalued company compared to industry, check its ROA and ROE. If ROA or ROE is anything decent (either over 5%) then forget it. This means the company is making some kind of money. No matter how little it may be, gamblers are less fearful knowing they are investing in a company that is generating some sort of earnings.

Next evaluate the percentage of shares shorted. If over 15% of the company's shares are shorted, disregard the stock. A high short ratio means that many investors are betting this company to be overvalued, which will make it all the harder for this stock to go down for two reasons:

First, there is a reduced potential for more short sellers to enter the stock to further drive down the price; and second, a spike in the stock price can start a vicious short squeeze, whereby the stock continues moving upward based on a deadly combination of shorts covering their position and greedy gamblers entering the stock.

The last metric is the stock's price trend. You want to find a company that is at, or close to, an all-time high with no justification for being that high; in other words a stock that has been pumped up by gambler speculation. These type of stocks have a huge spike up in a very short amount of time. On the contrary, stay away from stocks that have been slowly trending upwards. The slower the upward trend, the less likely that gamblers are fearful of a steep drop down.

Recall the gold mining chart discussed in Part III. There was a steady decline on low volume, and then eventually the price became so low that investors started disagreeing, evidenced by increasing volume and stabilizing prices. Use this same method to find an overvalued stock that investors are starting to think is overpriced. An upwards trend on low volume signifies little disagreement among investors. Once the trend begins slowing, and volume begins increasing, this shows that disagreement is beginning to brew.

You could also take a bearish position in a company that you believe will be insolvent soon. To do so, use the same criteria for identifying an overvalued stock. The only difference is that you are not looking for the most overvalued stock in an industry; instead, you are looking for an insolvent company that also happens to be overvalued. Insolvency first, overvalued second; however both must be present.

Why should a company be both insolvent and overvalued? An insolvent, *undervalued* company can still be acquired for a premium, while an insolvent, *overvalued* company will likely be acquired for less than its market value. You do not want to enter a bearish position at $0.50/share on an insolvent company that is worth $1/share, only to see an announcement a week later that it has been liquidated or acquired by another company at $1/share.

To assess a company's solvency, compare its Quick Ratio and Current Ratio to the industry. You want to select companies where one or both of these ratios are under 1, meaning the company has more current liabilities than current assets minus inventory (Quick Ratio), or more current liabilities than current assets (Current Ratio).

If these ratios are under 1, the company will have to obtain cash some sort of way in order to pay its bills.

The worst way (for you) is that the company expects to have increased earnings in the future. Increasing earnings will have a positive impact on the stock price.

A better way (for you) is that the company will incur more debt. Incurring more debt means the company's Quick Ratio and Current Ratio will decrease even more, plus the company will have to pay more interest charges each quarter, decreasing net income even further. However be cautioned that taking on additional debt can sometimes increase the stock price because it means the company has literally "bought time" to become profitable. If the company has a reasonable expectation to become profitable in the near future, then you want to stay away from entering a bearish position.

The best scenario is that the company issues more shares to raise capital. A company will choose to issue more shares if they do not want to, or usually cannot, take on any more debt.

This is most advantageous to you because stock prices should decrease after shares are issued; each share is now worth a smaller percentage of the company. Keep in mind that although a price decline is probable after issuing more shares, there is no guarantee that prices will decline. Perhaps the investment community believes that the additional capital will be the company's lifesaver, allowing the company to prosper in the long-term. In this situation, issuing more shares may convince gamblers that the company is more valuable than before.

Bearish positions are much more risky than bullish positions and must be entered with caution. You should purchase puts before shorting a stock. When purchasing puts the stock price has to drop past your premium cost before making a profit, however the stock should be significantly overvalued anyway so that a significant price drop is probable.

As previously mentioned, bearish positions should be used to hedge against a market crash – not to make money. You only want to exit a bearish position when both of these circumstances apply: 1) There is a better bearish opportunity elsewhere; 2) You will not lose money exiting your current position.

The only exception to this rule is that if an overvalued company suddenly becomes very profitable or undervalued. In this case you will want to exit, sometimes even with a loss, because it no longer meets your overvalued criteria.

You should not take 3% gains from bearish positions because it is difficult to find extremely overvalued companies relative to the market. Understand what I said here. It is easy to find overvalued companies in the market;

they are everywhere. However it is difficult to find companies that are significantly more overvalued than others.

If one day a company becomes significantly more overvalued than your current bearish positions, and you will not take a loss by exiting your bearish positions, then by all means make the switch.

By investing in strong, undervalued companies for your bullish positions, and extremely overvalued companies for your bearish positions, you will withstand unexpected market crashes much better than the average trader. Over the long-term, a market crash will only have a slight effect on undervalued companies compared to the huge effect it will have on overvalued companies. If you can smartly balance your bullish and bearish positions, it is possible to even profit from a market crash.

The last thing I want to mention is what I call "other fetishes." Other fetishes include all the complex option strategies, along with the other investment vehicles added in there: mutual funds, annuities, variable/fixed life insurance policies, savings plans, etc.

All these investment vehicles do have a place in the market, but that place is not my portfolio. Why? Because investment vehicle complexity usually equals higher risks or reduced returns. Examples: mutual funds relieve the investor of performing his own portfolio management in return for a slice of his profits; annuities take your money, invest it, then give it back to you in small increments; life insurance policies transfer the risk of death for a fee – you get the idea.

I am not denying the usefulness of these investments for others, but I am denying the usefulness for me and other insightful investors capable of actively managing their finances. If you are interested in these other investment vehicles then you should seek out an investment advisor (and I am wondering how you made it so far in this book).

Speaking of investment advisors, it is best to consult with them before making investment decisions, especially if you are new to investing. Everything I write about in this book is my own opinion and is not suitable for everyone. Grandma Gladis probably does not need to be analyzing and actively trading stocks with her social security checks.

Part V – Execution

I don't want my brother finishing your book with just his dick in his hands.

Strategy recap

We have covered a lot of information so far. Let us recap the investment strategy:

<u>For bullish positions (~90% of portfolio value):</u>

1) Identify volatile stocks that have favorable P/B, P/Cash, P/E, Current Ratio, ROA, and ROE compared to industry.

2) Give preference to those stocks that pay dividends, have recently taken huge dips, appear to be emerging from a long-term dip, primarily owned by insiders/institutions, not heavily shorted, growing earnings, do not have an underlying weakness, and are run by seemingly honest, competent management.

3) Weed out companies operating within uncertain industries (a VCR manufacturer may not be the wisest choice nowadays).

4) Partition your portfolio into 5-10% blocks; allocate a stock to each block, filling about 90% of your portfolio.

5) Enter a "Good Until Canceled" sell order with a limit price 3% over your cost basis.

For bearish positions (~10% of portfolio value):

1) Identify volatile stocks that have <u>un</u>favorable P/B, P/Cash, P/E, Current Ratio, ROA, and ROE compared to industry.

2) Give preference to those stocks with recent upward spikes, higher volume with smaller price increases, and all else opposite of selecting a bullish stock.

3) Weed out companies that are heavily shorted, companies with strong brand names, and companies operating in fast growing industries.

4) Purchase long-term puts for these stocks.

5) If the price falls 3% under your cost basis and there are better bearish stocks out there, execute put and immediately buy to cover your shorted shares. If your current bearish positions are the most overvalued in the market, then wait to execute put.

6) Do not deviate from your strategy out of fear or greed.

Realize there will be outstanding days where you increase your total portfolio by 10%, and there will be horrendous days where your unrealized losses hit 15% of portfolio value.

Also know that your current portfolio will always be painted red since you do not hold gains for long. This will be very hard for you to handle at first, and this feeling never goes away completely. There will be agonizing down days when you question your entire strategy.

If you can hang in there without making irrational decisions, your portfolio will soon recover. I have had days that started bad, but closed great. The stock market will continually fluctuate up and down. If the market happens to be hitting particularly hard one day, click over to your YTD gains/losses area. Here you will be reminded that your strategy is effective. In a year, when others have increased their portfolio by 15% of unrealized simple gains, you have increased your portfolio by 75% of realized compounded gains.

Remember to stick to your strategy; never deviate because of greed or fear. There will be times when you sell a stock 3% over cost basis and it later closes 10% over cost basis. Do not kick yourself over this, there will be more times when you sell a stock 3% over cost basis and it later closes *under* cost basis. Chasing gains out of greed is what the average trader does, and the average trader is not rich.

Practical execution

So you now have a straightforward plan to follow, and just need specific details on how to carry it out on a daily basis. I will describe my current process; you can either use mine or create one that best fits your style.

At the end of each day, I download stock data from www.finviz.com. This website provides very detailed stock data that is updated at the end of each trading day. I like this site because you can easily download their entire dataset without having to subscribe or submit yourself to advertisement waterboarding.

This site allows you to input your desired criteria in their stock screener, and saves it for future use. I have my screener bookmarked, so every day I just open the bookmark and click the "export" link to retrieve the data in Excel.

I copy and paste the exported data into an Excel workbook template that is setup on my local computer. This workbook has formulas that automatically update once new data is copied in. These formulas calculate each company's standings compared to their industries (for example, to determine if a particular stock is over or undervalued when comparing their P/B to industry). You can download my Excel template for free by visiting www.predictingsociety.com.

After formulas are recalculated based on today's data, pivot tables show the most undervalued and overvalued stocks on the market. These pivot tables allow me to compare all undervalued and overvalued stocks against each other. I glance at the pivot tables to see if any new stocks are showing up as under or overvalued. If so, I'll research the company using Yahoo! Finance. If it meets all criteria described in this book, I add it to my online brokerage watch list.

My watch list is sorted to show percentage losses for the day, in descending order. It also has the company's ask and bid price, 50-day moving average, and percentage away from the 52-week high.

When the market opens, I watch to see which undervalued stocks fall the quickest and fastest. The further down a stock falls, with no news to substantiate it, the more attractive purchase it is. For instance, any strong company that falls 10% at the market open for no reason (other than a bunch of people sold at low prices at once) is a prime acquisition target. I usually buy into these companies immediately.

Buys are performed using limit orders only. Never buy into a stock using a market order; market orders can kill your chances of selling at a quick 3% gain. Consider the situation where you find an undervalued stock selling at $2/share and enter a market order to buy 2000 shares. If there are only 500 shares available at $2, and the rest are available at $2.10, then you have just purchased 1500 shares at $2.10 – a 5% premium. Your once undervalued stock is not so undervalued anymore.

If all companies are up for the day and cannot be bought for a reasonable price at or below their 50-day moving average, then I usually abstain from entering any positions. It will not be long before one of these stocks fall a few percent, and I would rather be buying after, not before, it falls. Avoid the temptation to invest money just because you have it on hand. Wait for the right opportunity.

Immediately after purchasing the stock, I set a sell limit order for 3% over my cost basis. Rinse and repeat.

Realize the immense value of this strategy. Maintaining a pre-researched set of stocks in your watch list means you are not out there irrationally buying whichever stock you happen to come across that day. You have done all the research beforehand and compiled a list of most undervalued stocks. Now you are just looking for an entry opportunity. By using this strategy of selecting the best of the best stocks, you have double protected yourself from loss and placed yourself at an advantage from the get-go.

Closing comments

We have covered many concepts in this book, so let us recap things.

In the short-term, stocks randomly move up and down over a certain baseline. Buying an already undervalued stock below its baseline means you are getting in at a very opportune point.

Too many people chase stocks upward. If they have been watching a stock and one day it shoots up, they impulsively buy in at a high point because they do not want to feel as if they missed an easy gain.

Time after time after time again I have witnessed stocks shoot up, then come crashing right down. The winners are those that bought in at a low price and sold with a modest gain; the losers are those that chased the price up, only to see it fall back down again.

Once you are into a stock position, immediately enter your 3% sell order. Do not fall into the trap that so many do, thinking you have found the one stock that is destined to go up 20% from the very moment you bought it.

No matter how undervalued the stock is, there is no guarantee that it will realize its true value anytime soon. Consider, how did the stock become so undervalued to begin with? It went from fairly priced, to slightly undervalued, to moderately undervalued, to significantly undervalued. You could have bought in at any of these phases, thinking the stock was undervalued and destined to go back up to fair price, and each time you would have been wrong. You would have held the stock and simply watched it decrease in value over time.

No matter how undervalued the stock appears, remember that you are not a fortuneteller. You cannot predict how it is going to move. So set your 3% sell order and go on with your life.

The more an undervalued stock drops in a day, with no substantiating news, the better buy-in opportunity it is. Therefore if I see one of the stocks on my watch list suddenly drop 10% for no reason at all, I jump right in.

There are times when I am fully invested and cannot jump right in. In these instances, I may sell one of my existing stocks for less than a 3% gain; however I practically never sell for less than a 2% gain.

Just as it is okay to execute a put if you find a more overvalued stock out there, it is okay to sell a bullish position for a gain if there is a much better opportunity elsewhere.

You have to be objective as possible when selling stocks for less than a 3% gain. Traders, the frantic people that they are, have a tendency to prematurely sell and buy. This tendency causes people to sell for a loss, in search of greener pastures. After switching for a loss, it is possible that his older stock increases while his new stock drops.

Never sell without a darn good reason. Darn good reason #1: The stock appreciated 3% over your cost basis. Darn good reason #2: You are able to enter into an undervalued stock that experienced a huge dip, while still making a decent profit on your current position. Darn good reason #3: The company was impacted by a significantly negative event which made it no longer undervalued.

There is no darn good reason #4.

What if you have free money to invest, yet no stocks have dropped during the day? Then do not invest; wait until a stock drops.

The market moves up and down in waves. This means that if the market is significantly up today, chances are it will drop tomorrow. And if it drops tomorrow, chances are it will rise the day after.

Never buy stocks that are up for the day, no matter how much you are kicking yourself for not getting in sooner. Just like Rocky Balboa, you will get your shot. It does not matter which stock you get a shot in. All that matters is you bought and sold for a profit.

My goal with this book was to provide valuable and practical insight to you, the reader, so that you could retire in four years and live off smart investments, then become a billionaire later if you choose to do so.

Life is too short and too precious to spend it at a workplace 40+ hours a week. Take control of your life by disciplining yourself to become rich in the market.

The more money you smartly invest in the market, the larger and faster it will grow. Therefore, to get rich, you need to invest as much as possible, as early as possible. Pay extra on the house note? No, put it in the market. Just got a bonus at work? Put it in the market. Maintain a savings account in case the market drops? No, put it in the market. Go on an expensive vacation? No, put it in the market.

You have to make sacrifices early in order to obtain rewards later.

This concept is often misunderstood, though. Many people sacrifice their entire life, setting aside money in a savings account, then retiring and enjoying a modest living at 65. They were eventually able to retire without worrying about work again, but at what cost? They sacrificed their 40 best years for a somewhat comfortable 20 years.

You, armed with the knowledge of an insightful investor, can deploy a different strategy. Get a good education in your late teens and early 20s, then get a good paying job. Use your salary to continually feed your portfolio, compounding your money in the stock market.

Strive for raises and promotions – not to buy a new vehicle, but to invest more into the market. Spend your weekends thinking how you can earn more money. Find your launching pad and pursue it during your off-time. Put the proceeds from your launching pad into the market.

If you are disciplined enough to stay on track, your daily market gains will begin exceeding your daily salary from work. When this happens, you will know that you are getting close to the finish line.

Stay focused and objective, and soon you will reach the point where your work salary does not mean much anymore. Compared to your daily stock market gains, your work salary appears more like that $20 envelope that you receive every year on your birthday. You find that, by retiring from work, you can easily live off your daily market gains, while still compounding your portfolio. In fact, you actually become a better trader at home because you can devote more time to it.

This is the sweet spot you have waited for – the time that you can retire from your job. The same sweet spot that takes most 40 years to reach, takes you about 4 years to reach. You are able to retire at a young age and live your life as you choose.

Thank you for supporting my launching pad. You now have the tools required to become rich in the market. They are not complicated, however many traders still do not understand these tools or purposely ignore them with the false pretense that greater stock analysis complexity equals greater returns. Exotic trading strategies do not equal better returns in the market; if they did, then there would have been a computer algorithm invented long ago. Becoming rich in the market requires a tool that most people do not possess – making rational decisions by controlling their emotions.

I sincerely hope that you are now able to break free from society's constraints and move towards achieving your life goals.

You are the success of my launching pad. If you think I have changed your life with this book, please a leave an insightful review on the Internet, and spread word to your friends and family who invest in the market. Your review alone can result in 10,000 additional book sales, seriously.

Thank you for your time

A Dedication to the Misc

A special thanks goes out to the Bodybuilding.com Misc. forum for giving me years of laughs and interesting social commentaries; and most importantly – for promoting this book across the world. You helped make it a success.

I specifically want to thank these cheeky Miscers:

standon23
Inhumanity – *"Best of luck to you and your fantasy of being a stock billionaire."*
apo99
tunyce
Rawrs. – *"Fluorine uranium carbon potassium bismuth technetium helium sulfur germanium thulium oxygen neon yttrium."*
TaxPayingTongan
GetBigBrag – *"Disregard sloots, aquire currency and aesthetics."*
shaboy211
Mav3535 – *"Healthy skeptic."*
KoCorl – *"There is no tool in this pool."*
NattyCory – *"Buy heavy, Take your multivitamin, and make all kinds of gains."*
Kuzon – *"I will use this book to achieve CEO 10k a day."*

The End

6504799R00084

Printed in Great Britain
by Amazon.co.uk, Ltd.,
Marston Gate.